Her Man, His Secret

Robyn Bailey

HER MAN, HIS SECRET

Understanding the Down Low Men

Who Pursue Trans Women, Femboys & Drag Queens

Robyn Bailey

Her Man, His Secret: Understanding the Down Low Men
Who Pursue Trans Women, Femboys & Drag Queens

This is a work of nonfiction. The stories and experiences presented in this book are based on real people, real interviews, and real research. Some names and identifying details have been changed or composited to protect the privacy of individuals. The author has made every effort to ensure the accuracy of the information presented, while honoring the lived experiences of those who shared their stories.

Published by Eye for Change Consulting, Inc.
Cleveland, Ohio

ISBN: 978-0-9890946-3-4

Cover design by Eye for Change Consulting, Inc.
Interior layout and typesetting by Eye for Change Consulting, Inc.

First Edition

Printed in the United States of America

10 9 8 7 6 5 4 3 2 1

*To every woman who ever looked in the mirror and wondered
if she was losing her mind—you weren't.*

*To every trans woman, femboy, and drag queen
who loved someone who could never love you in the light—
you deserved better.*

*To every man still hiding in the shadows—
may you find the courage to step out of them.*

*And to my grandmother, Daisy Mae Russell,
who taught me that the truth—no matter how hard—
is always worth telling.*

Contents

CHAPTER ONE

Redefining the Down Low: It's Not All the Same

Let me start by being completely honest with you. If you picked up this book, you already know something is wrong. Maybe you felt it in your gut when he tilted his phone away from you at the dinner table. Maybe you noticed that his eyes lingered a beat too long on someone who wasn't quite who you expected. Maybe a friend pulled you aside and whispered something that made your stomach drop. Or maybe you've already found the evidence, the messages, the photos, the dating profile on an app you'd never heard of, and now you're holding this book because you need someone to tell you the truth about what you're dealing with.

I'm going to tell you that truth. And I'm going to tell it to you as somebody who has a foot in every world this book touches. I'm Black. I'm a member of the LGBTQIA community. I grew up in the same churches, sat at the same dinner tables, and navigated the same cultural expectations that shape the men and women in these pages. I'm not writing about this from the outside looking in. I'm writing from the inside, from a place of love for my community, respect for the women who are hurting, and understanding for the men who are hiding. That doesn't mean I'm here to make excuses. It means I'm here to tell the whole truth, including the parts that make everybody uncomfortable.

And here's the first uncomfortable truth: not all down low behavior is the same. That distinction, the one that nobody talks about, is the reason this book exists.

For over twenty years, the phrase "on the down low" has carried a singular meaning in popular culture: a man who sleeps with other men in secret while presenting as heterosexual to the world. That's the story America was told. That's the narrative that launched a thousand talk show segments, church sermons, barbershop arguments, and late-night conversations between women wondering if they really know the man sleeping next to them. And while that narrative isn't wrong, it is dangerously incomplete.

Because within the world of men living on the down low, there exists a massive, unexamined divide. On one side are men who are sexually and romantically attracted to other masculine-presenting men, men who look like men, dress like men, and carry themselves like men. On the other side are men who are specifically and often exclusively attracted to trans women, femboys, and drag queens, individuals who wear the hair, the nails, who are smooth-shaven from head to toe, and who look, dress, and present as women in every visible way.

These are not the same thing. And understanding the difference is not just an academic exercise. For the woman sitting in her living room right now, trying to make sense of what she's discovered, understanding this difference could change how she processes her pain, how she understands her man, and ultimately, how she decides to move forward.

How We Got Here: The Story America Was Told

To understand where the down low conversation went sideways, you have to go back to the early 2000s, when the phrase went from street slang to national headline. Now, if you're Black and over thirty-five, you already know this history because you lived it. The term "down low" or "DL" had been floating around our communities for years: we heard it in the barbershop, at the cookout, whispered between aunties at the family reunion. R&B and hip-hop culture gave it a soundtrack, R. Kelly, TLC in the mid-1990s. But it didn't become a mainstream cultural phenomenon, meaning white America started paying attention, until two pivotal events happened almost back to back.

The first was a feature article in The New York Times Magazine in August 2003, written by journalist Benoit Denizet-Lewis. Now, I have to keep it real here, there was always something that sat sideways about the fact that it took an openly gay white journalist to bring our community's business to the front page of The New York Times Magazine. But that's exactly what happened. Denizet-Lewis profiled Black men across the country who were secretly having sex with other men while maintaining relationships with women, and he brought the concept of the down low to a national, predominantly white audience for the first time. He painted a portrait of a hidden subculture operating in plain sight, men meeting in parks, gyms, and through early internet chat rooms, engaging in sexual encounters that their wives and girlfriends knew nothing about. The article connected this behavior directly to the rising rates of HIV among Black women, framing DL men as an invisible vector of transmission. And just like that, our dirty laundry was front-page news.

The second, and far more explosive, event was J. L. King.

In April 2004, King appeared on The Oprah Winfrey Show to promote his book, On the Down Low: A Journey into the Lives of "Straight" Black Men Who Sleep with Men. The episode was a cultural earthquake. King, a married father from Springfield, Ohio, sat across from Oprah and calmly explained that he had been sleeping with men throughout his entire marriage, sometimes in his own home, while his wife slept upstairs, and that he was far from alone. He told Oprah and her millions of viewers that countless men were living this double life, and that the women in their lives had no idea they were at risk.

King's book became a massive bestseller. His Oprah appearance remains one of the most-discussed episodes in the show's history. And I don't have to tell you what happened next; because if you're a Black woman of a certain age, you remember. Every phone in America was ringing. Every group chat, well, we didn't have group chats yet, but every three-way call, was lit up. Your mama called you. Your girlfriend from college called you. The women at your church were whispering about it in the fellowship hall. Almost overnight, every Black woman in America was looking at her man a little differently.

But here's what got lost in the explosion of media coverage, church sermons, and girlfriends' group chat conversations that followed: the down low was presented as a single, monolithic thing. Man sleeps with man in secret. Period. End of story.

The nuances were buried. The distinctions were ignored. And the most significant distinction of all: the one between men attracted to masculine men and men attracted to feminine-presenting individuals, was never even raised.

Denise's Story

Denise was a thirty-eight-year-old paralegal in Atlanta when she found the first clue. Her husband, Marcus, had left his iPad on the kitchen counter, and when she picked it up to move it, the screen lit up to a text conversation with someone named "Kiki." The profile picture showed a stunningly beautiful woman with long, flowing hair, perfect makeup, and acrylic nails. Denise's first reaction was anger: the kind of anger any woman feels when she realizes her man is talking to another woman. She screenshotted the conversation and confronted Marcus that night.

But when Marcus broke down and told her the truth, Denise's world shifted in a way she never expected. Kiki was a trans woman. Marcus had been seeing her for almost two years. They went on dates. He bought her gifts. He told Kiki things about his childhood he'd never told Denise. And when Denise asked him the question that was burning in her chest, "Are you gay?", Marcus looked at her with genuine confusion and said, "No. She's a woman to me."

Denise didn't know what to do with that answer. Everything she'd read about the down low told her that her husband was a closeted gay man. But what she was looking at, the pictures, the conversations, the dynamic, didn't look like what she'd been told to look for. It looked like a heterosexual affair, except the other woman happened to be trans.

Denise's experience is far more common than most people realize. And her confusion: that feeling of the ground shifting beneath her feet because the situation didn't match the narrative she'd been given, is exactly why this book needed to be written.

The Framework That Failed Us

The problem with how America talks about the down low is that we've been using a framework built in 2004 to understand a reality that is far more complex in 2026. And as somebody who lives in this community, who has sat with DL men, prayed with their wives, broken bread with trans women who date them, and watched the whole messy, painful ecosystem up close, I can tell you that framework was never sufficient to begin with. When J. L. King went on Oprah, the conversation was almost exclusively framed around Black men who have sex with other men, MSM, as public health researchers call them. The health angle dominated everything. The Centers for Disease Control and Prevention had been sounding alarms about HIV transmission rates among Black women, and the DL narrative provided a convenient explanation: our women were getting infected because our men were secretly sleeping with other men and bringing the virus home.

And there was real data behind that fear. According to CDC surveillance reports, the vast majority of HIV diagnoses among Black women, approximately ninety percent, have been attributed to heterosexual transmission. Black women accounted for roughly half of all new HIV diagnoses among women in the United States, despite representing only about thirteen percent of the female population. These are staggering numbers, and they deserve serious attention.

But the DL narrative as it was told to the public was a blunt instrument. And I say this as someone in the LGBTQIA community who watched it happen in real time: the mainstream media and the public health establishment took an enormously complex web of factors, systemic poverty, mass incarceration that disrupted sexual networks in our communities, lack of access to healthcare, higher background prevalence of STIs, stigma that prevented testing; and reduced it all to a single boogeyman: the DL man. He became the monster under the bed. The invisible threat. And in doing so, the narrative did something else that was equally damaging: it told every woman that any man living a secret sexual life outside the heterosexual norm was, fundamentally, the same kind of threat. It also, by the way, further demonized queer Black men in a community that was already hostile to them; but that's a conversation for another chapter.

He's not. And here's where I need you to really lean in, because this is the part nobody else is saying.

The Divide Nobody Talks About

Picture two men. We'll call them David and Terrence. Both are married to women. Both are fathers. Both present themselves as straight to their families, their friends, their coworkers, and their communities. Both are living what the world would call a "down low" lifestyle. But the similarities end there.

David downloads hookup apps that cater to men seeking men. He creates a faceless profile, just a torso pic, and arranges quick, anonymous encounters with other men. Sometimes it's in a car. Sometimes it's at the other man's apartment. The men David meets are masculine-presenting. Some are married themselves. There is no romance, no dating, no emotional connection. David would never be seen in public with any of these men in any context that could be misconstrued. Afterward, he deletes the app, showers, and goes home to his wife as if nothing happened. David's attraction is to men as men. The masculinity is part of the appeal.

Terrence's secret life looks entirely different. Terrence is drawn to trans women, specifically, trans women who have invested heavily in their feminine presentation. Long hair, flawless makeup, manicured nails, smooth skin, curves, and clothing that would make any woman in the mall envious. When Terrence scrolls through social media late at night, he's not looking at men. He's looking at women, women who happen to be trans. He follows Instagram models who document their transitions and their beauty routines. He's on dating apps, but not the ones David uses. Terrence is on platforms that cater specifically to men interested in trans women. And unlike David, Terrence's encounters are not always quick and anonymous. He takes his partners out. He texts them throughout the day. He buys them things. In many cases, Terrence is engaged in what looks, from the outside, exactly like a heterosexual relationship; because for him, that's what it feels like.

Now, here's my question for you, the reader: Are David and Terrence the same? Are they motivated by the same thing? Are they hiding the same secret? Is the experience of the woman married to David the same as the experience of the woman married to Terrence?

The answer, if we're being honest, is no. And the fact that our culture has lumped these two very different men into the same category for over twenty years has done a disservice to everyone involved, especially the women trying to make sense of what they're dealing with.

What the Science Actually Tells Us

If you're reading this and thinking, "This sounds like you're just making excuses for these men," I want to pause right here and tell you: that's not what this is. Understanding is not excusing. Explanation is not justification. Your pain is real regardless of the label we put on his behavior. But if you're going to navigate this situation wisely, you need accurate information, not just the information that confirms what you already think.

Here's what the science tells us. Researchers at Northwestern University published a groundbreaking series of studies examining men who are sexually attracted to trans women. The clinical term for this attraction is gynandromorphophilia, or GAMP. The researchers, led by Kevin J. Hsu and J. Michael Bailey, conducted both laboratory studies measuring physical arousal and large-scale internet surveys of hundreds of these men.

Their findings were striking. Men attracted to trans women showed arousal patterns that were far more similar to heterosexual men than to gay men. Their physical responses to masculine stimuli were low, comparable to straight men's responses. But their responses to feminine-presenting trans individuals were high, sometimes matching their responses to cisgender women. The researchers concluded that this attraction pattern is best understood as an unusual variant of heterosexuality rather than as homosexuality or bisexuality. In one 2017 study published in the *Archives of Sexual Behavior*, the researchers surveyed 314 men with this attraction and found they reported much higher attraction to women than to men, though they did show slightly elevated bisexual feelings compared to control groups.

Let me say that again for the women in the back: the scientific evidence suggests that men who are attracted to trans women are not, as a group, closeted gay men. Their brains, their bodies, their arousal patterns are responding to femininity. The fact that the feminine person they're attracted to happens to be trans rather than cisgender doesn't flip some switch that makes them gay. It makes them men who are attracted to a different expression of the femininity they're already wired to respond to.

This doesn't mean the behavior isn't hurtful. This doesn't mean the secrecy is acceptable. This doesn't mean you shouldn't be furious. But it does mean that if you're trying to understand what's happening with your man, calling him gay and leaving it at that might not just be inaccurate: it might actually prevent you from understanding the real situation.

Patricia's Story

Patricia found out about her husband Michael's secret life in the worst possible way: a friend sent her a screenshot. The image was from a local social media page, and it showed Michael at a restaurant with a woman Patricia had never seen: a tall, glamorous woman in a bodycon dress with long, lace-front hair and flawless contour makeup. Patricia's friend had recognized Michael in the background of someone else's photo. When she zoomed in, there was no question: it was him, leaning across the table, holding this woman's hand.

Patricia confronted Michael, expecting him to say it was a coworker, a cousin, anything. Instead, he went silent for a long time and then told her the truth: the woman's name was Jade, she was a trans woman, and they had been seeing each other for almost a year. Patricia's first instinct was to scream, "So you're gay!" Michael's response rocked her: "Look at her. Does she look like a man to you? I'm not attracted to men. I've never been attracted to men. I'm attracted to her because she's beautiful and feminine and she makes me feel something."

Patricia didn't know how to categorize what was happening. If she told her mother, her mother would say Michael was gay. If she told her best friend, her best friend would say the same thing. But what Patricia saw with her own eyes, the photos, the text messages full of "baby" and "I miss you," the dinner dates, looked like an affair with a woman. A beautiful woman. Just one who happened to be transgender.

"The hardest part," Patricia told me, "was that I couldn't even hate her. I looked her up on Instagram. She was gorgeous. She had thousands of followers. She wasn't some secret he was ashamed of: he was the secret. She didn't even know he was married."

Sexual Orientation vs. Attraction to Gender Presentation

One of the biggest conceptual traps women fall into when trying to understand DL behavior is the binary framework of gay versus straight. Our culture teaches us that there are two categories: you're either attracted to the opposite sex or you're attracted to the same sex. If a man is sleeping with someone who was born male, he must be gay. Case closed.

But human sexuality has never been that simple, and the rise of visible trans women, femboys, and drag queens in mainstream culture has exposed just how inadequate that framework is. Here's a different way to think about it that might help.

Sexual orientation, whether someone is gay, straight, or bisexual, is typically understood as attraction to a biological sex. But what actually triggers attraction in the real world, on a moment-to-moment basis, is not chromosomes or birth certificates. It's presentation. It's what you see, what you smell, what you feel. When a man sees a person with long, flowing hair, smooth skin, a feminine face, curves, manicured nails, and a dress that hugs in all the right places, his brain doesn't run a DNA test before deciding whether he's attracted. His brain responds to what's in front of him. And what's in front of him looks like a woman.

For men like Terrence and Michael, the attraction is rooted in femininity itself, not in the biological sex of the person presenting it. A masculine-presenting man holds zero appeal for them. A woman in sweats with no makeup? They're attracted. A trans woman who has invested in creating a hyper-feminine appearance? They're attracted. A femboy with silky smooth skin, painted nails, and a soft, feminine energy? They're attracted. What all these objects of attraction have in common is femininity, not femaleness.

This is not a minor distinction. For the woman trying to understand her man, this is the entire ballgame. If your man is attracted to masculine men, men who present as men, then you are dealing with a form of same-sex attraction that he is hiding. That is its own complicated reality, and it deserves its own honest conversation. But if your man is attracted to individuals who look, dress, smell, and carry themselves like women, who have invested thousands of dollars and countless hours into achieving a feminine presentation that would fool most people on the street, then you are dealing with something different. Something that is, in many ways, more complicated and more confusing, but also fundamentally different in it's psychological and emotional DNA.

The Elephant in the Room: What the Internet Reveals

If you want to understand the scale of what we're talking about, you don't need a psychology textbook. You just need to look at the data that the internet generates every single day.

Pornhub, the world's largest adult entertainment platform, publishes annual reports analyzing viewing trends across its billions of users. The data is staggering. In 2022, transgender content on the platform surged by seventy-five percent, making it the seventh most popular category worldwide and the third most popular in the United States. By 2023, it had climbed to sixth most viewed globally. And in the platform's most recent data, transgender content rose another fifty-eight percent to become the second most viewed category on the entire site.

The scale of this trend cannot be overstated. On a platform visited by hundreds of millions of people. This is not a niche interest. This is not a fringe curiosity. This is a massive, mainstream phenomenon that is hiding in plain sight; and the overwhelming majority of these viewers are men who, in their daily lives, identify as heterosexual.

The data also reveals something else that's important for the conversation in this book: the interest spans all age groups. Men between twenty-five and forty-four showed the highest consumption rates, but viewership was significant across every demographic. These are not confused teenagers experimenting online. These are grown men, husbands, fathers, boyfriends, deacons, coaches, executives, who are privately consuming content featuring trans women and feminine-presenting individuals at rates that would shock the women in their lives.

I bring this up not to shame anyone's private viewing habits, but to make a critical point: the man who is attracted to trans women or femboys is not some rare anomaly. He is not a one-in-a-million outlier. He is everywhere. He is at your job. He is at your church. He may be at your kitchen table right now. And the fact that we as a culture have never had an honest conversation about this particular form of attraction, lumping it instead into the same category as men who are attracted to other men, has left millions of women without the tools they need to understand their own reality.

Tonya's Story

Tonya was a forty-two-year-old schoolteacher in Houston. She'd been married to Robert for sixteen years. They had two children, a mortgage, and what she called "a boring, beautiful life." The discovery happened by accident. Robert had asked Tonya to look something up on his laptop while he was in the shower. When she opened the browser, the last tab was still active: a dating profile on an app Tonya had never heard of. The profile listed Robert as a "straight man seeking trans women."

Tonya sat on the edge of the bed and stared at the screen until the words blurred. Robert's profile was detailed. He described himself as "a real man who appreciates real femininity." He listed his preferences: "fem, passable, long hair, smooth." His messages to women on the app were flirtatious, complimentary, and, this was the part that gutted Tonya, romantic. He wasn't looking for a quick encounter in a parking lot. He was looking for connection.

When Tonya confronted Robert, he didn't deny it. But he refused to accept the label she tried to put on him. "I'm not gay," he told her. "I'm not even bi. I don't look at men. I don't want men. I want women. Some of the women I'm attracted to happen to be trans. That's it."

Tonya later told me, "The thing that messed me up the most was that I couldn't argue with him. I saw the women on that app. They were beautiful. If you showed me their pictures without telling me they were trans, I would have just thought they were pretty women. So was he wrong? Was he gay for finding them attractive? I honestly didn't know."

J. L. King Revisited: What He Got Right and What He Missed

I want to return to J. L. King for a moment, because his story is actually a perfect illustration of the very confusion this book is trying to clear up.

When King appeared on Oprah in 2004, he was emphatic about one thing: he was not gay. He rejected the label entirely. He told Oprah and her audience that DL men were not closeted homosexuals: they were men who had sex with men but whose identity, self-image, and primary attraction remained rooted in their relationships with women. King drew a hard line between DL behavior and gayness, and he insisted that America needed to understand the difference.

Six years later, in 2010, King returned to Oprah's show and made a stunning reversal. He acknowledged that he was, in fact, a gay man. He had been in denial for decades, and his insistence that he wasn't gay had been part of that denial. His ex-wife, Brenda Stone Browder, sat beside him as he made this admission, and she later wrote her own book, Diary of a Cover Girl, documenting the devastation of discovering her husband's double life.

King's reversal was significant. But it also, inadvertently, cemented a narrative that has done lasting damage: the idea that every DL man is just a gay man in denial, and that if you wait long enough, the truth will come out. For many DL men, that narrative is accurate. King was attracted to men. He was gay. His denial was a defense mechanism built by homophobia, religion, family expectations, and the fear of losing everything.

But King's story is not every man's story. And the critical mistake our culture has made is applying King's arc, DL man denies being gay, eventually admits he's gay, as a universal template for all DL behavior. For the man who is exclusively attracted to hyper-feminine trans women and has never once been aroused by a masculine man, that template doesn't fit. And forcing it to fit doesn't help you. It just keeps you confused.

Why the Language Matters

I know some readers might be thinking, "Why does it matter what we call it? He's still cheating. He's still lying. He's still putting me at risk." And you're absolutely right. The betrayal is real no matter what label we stick on it. If your man is carrying on a secret relationship with anyone, trans woman, cisgender woman, man, or anyone else, he has violated your trust, and that violation doesn't become more or less painful based on the gender identity of his affair partner.

But here's why the language matters anyway: because the language shapes the response. And the wrong response can make a devastating situation even worse.

When a woman discovers that her husband or boyfriend is involved with another cisgender woman, the path forward, while painful, is culturally scripted. She knows what she's dealing with. She can talk to her mother, her sister, her best friend, her pastor, or her therapist, and they all have a framework for understanding what happened and helping her process it.

When a woman discovers that her man is involved with a masculine-presenting man, the cultural script shifts to another familiar framework: he's gay, he's been lying, you need to get tested, and you need to leave. Painful, but culturally comprehensible.

But when a woman discovers that her man is involved with a trans woman who looks like a Victoria's Secret model? When she looks at the pictures and sees someone who is undeniably feminine, undeniably beautiful, and not what she expected? The cultural script breaks down entirely. She doesn't know what to call it. She doesn't know who to tell. She doesn't know if her man is gay, straight, bisexual, or something she doesn't have a word for. And that confusion, that inability to categorize what's happening, compounds the pain of the betrayal with the paralysis of not knowing how to even begin to process it.

That's what this book is for. It's not a manual for excusing bad behavior. It's a manual for understanding what you're actually facing, so you can make decisions from a place of clarity rather than confusion.

Keisha's Story

Keisha was twenty-nine and had been with her boyfriend, Andre, for five years when she found out. She was doing laundry and a receipt fell out of Andre's jacket pocket. It was from a high-end wig shop: a purchase for a thirty-inch Brazilian body wave lace front that cost over four hundred dollars. Keisha didn't wear wigs. When she asked Andre about it, he fumbled through an explanation about buying it for his cousin. But the cousin denied it.

What Keisha uncovered over the next two weeks shattered everything she thought she knew. Andre had been in a relationship with a femboy named Dion: a twenty-three-year-old who went by "Dee" on social media. Dee's Instagram was filled with photos showing a slender figure in feminine clothing, flawless skin, long nails, and the exact type of wig Andre had purchased. Dee's presentation was entirely feminine, you would never know from a photo that Dee was assigned male at birth.

Keisha went through every stage of grief in a matter of days. But the stage she got stuck on was confusion. "Everybody I tried to talk to just said, 'He's gay, leave him,'" she told me. "But when I looked at Dee's page, I saw a woman. A young, pretty woman. Andre wasn't looking at men. He wasn't on Grindr. He was on apps where men meet trans women and femboys. And the way he talked about Dee in his messages: it was exactly how he talked to me when we first started dating. The same compliments. The same energy. It was like he was dating a woman."

Keisha's confusion is the norm, not the exception. And her frustration at being given the standard "he's gay" response when her lived experience told her something more complicated was happening: that frustration is shared by more women than anyone realizes.

The Spectrum You Were Never Told About

Part of the reason this conversation is so difficult is that we lack the vocabulary for it. Our culture gives us neat boxes: gay, straight, bisexual. But the reality of human attraction doesn't fit neatly into boxes, and the men this book focuses on are living proof.

Think of attraction not as a light switch, on or off, gay or straight, but as a spectrum with femininity on one end and masculinity on the other. Most straight men are clustered at the femininity end: they are attracted to feminine-presenting people, full stop. Most gay men are clustered at the masculinity end: they are attracted to masculine-presenting people. Bisexual men are attracted to both ends of the spectrum to varying degrees.

The men this book is about exist in a specific zone on that spectrum. They are attracted to femininity, powerfully, consistently, and often exclusively. But their definition of femininity extends beyond cisgender women to include anyone who presents as convincingly feminine: trans women who have transitioned and invested in their feminine presentation, femboys who embrace a soft and feminine aesthetic, and drag queens whose transformation into glamorous women creates an object of genuine desire. These men are not attracted to masculinity in any form. Put a masculine-presenting man in front of them and they feel nothing. Put a feminine-presenting person in front of them, regardless of what's on that person's birth certificate, and their brains light up exactly the way they do when they see a cisgender woman.

This doesn't make their behavior acceptable if it's hidden and dishonest. Nothing in this book is an argument for secrecy or betrayal. But it does mean that when you're processing what your man has done, you owe it to yourself to process the accurate version of what happened, not a version filtered through a framework that was built for a different situation.

The Role of Culture, Community, and Shame

Before we move on, there's another layer to this conversation that has to be addressed, and it's one that sits at the intersection of race, religion, masculinity, and community expectations. The down low phenomenon has historically been discussed most prominently within the Black community, and while DL behavior exists across every racial and ethnic group, and this book speaks to women of every background, it would be dishonest to ignore the cultural forces that have shaped how this conversation has unfolded.

In our communities, and I say "our" intentionally, because this is my community too, the pressure on men to perform a specific kind of masculinity is intense. I've watched it my whole life. That masculinity is tied to strength, stoicism, heterosexual dominance, and an unwavering commitment to being seen as "a man's man." The Black church, which has been the cultural and spiritual backbone of our communities for generations, has often reinforced these expectations with teachings that frame any deviation from heterosexual norms as sinful, shameful, and worthy of condemnation. Now, I love the Black church. I was raised in it. I understand the role it plays in our survival, our joy, and our identity. But I also have to be honest about the harm it has done to LGBTQIA people, including the men this book is about. For a Black man who discovers he is attracted to trans women or femboys, the prospect of having that attraction exposed can feel like social annihilation. He would lose not just his reputation, but potentially his family, his church community, his friendships, and his sense of self.

This is not an excuse. It is context. And context matters because it explains why so many men choose secrecy over honesty. It explains why a man might maintain a picture-perfect heterosexual life while conducting an entirely separate emotional and sexual existence in the shadows. And it explains why, for many women, the discovery comes as such a devastating shock; because the man's public performance was so convincing that even the people closest to him had no idea.

The shame machine works differently depending on which type of DL behavior we're talking about. A man who is secretly sleeping with other masculine-presenting men faces the specific stigma of homosexuality: the fear of being labeled gay in a community that may treat that label as the ultimate emasculation. A man who is secretly involved with trans women or femboys faces a different but overlapping set of fears. He's terrified of the confusion his revelation would cause: people wouldn't just call him gay, they'd call him weird, confused, a freak. The taboo around attraction to trans women carries its own unique brand of social punishment, one that sits in a no-man's-land between homophobia and transphobia.

I've sat across the table from men on both sides of this divide, in living rooms, in coffee shops, in church parking lots after service, and the language they use to describe their fear is remarkably different. Brothers attracted to other men often say things like, "I can't let people know I'm into dudes." Brothers attracted to trans women say things like, "I can't let people know I'm into 'that.'" The word "that" carries enormous weight: it reflects a culture that hasn't even given these men a socially acceptable way to describe what they're attracted to, let alone a safe space to be open about it. And as somebody in the LGBTQIA community, I can tell you that even within our spaces, spaces that are supposed to be inclusive and accepting, the men who are attracted to trans women and femboys often feel like they don't have a home. They're not embraced by the gay community because they don't identify as gay. They're rejected by the straight world because their attraction doesn't fit the mold. They exist in a no-man's-land, and that isolation feeds the secrecy.

For you, the woman reading this, the takeaway is simple but important: the secrecy your man has been living in is not just about you. It's not just about his character or his morality. It's about an entire system of cultural pressure that makes honesty feel impossible for him. That doesn't make his dishonesty acceptable. But it does help explain it. And explanation, as I said earlier, is the first step toward making decisions from a place of power rather than confusion.

Vanessa's Story

Vanessa grew up in the church. Her father was a deacon. Her husband, Jerome, was the worship leader. They were the couple everyone pointed to as relationship goals. When Vanessa discovered Jerome's Instagram burner account: an account where he followed dozens of trans women and femboy influencers, and had exchanged flirtatious DMs with at least three of them, her first call wasn't to a friend or a therapist. It was to her pastor.

The pastor told Vanessa that Jerome was dealing with a "spirit of homosexuality" and that the answer was prayer, fasting, and deliverance sessions. Jerome was called into the pastor's office. He was prayed over. He was told to delete the account and never look at "that kind of thing" again. Jerome complied, publicly. Within three months, Vanessa discovered he had created a new account on a different platform.

"The church couldn't help me," Vanessa said, "because the church didn't understand what we were dealing with. They treated it like Jerome was a closeted gay man who just needed to pray harder. But Jerome wasn't looking at men. He was looking at women who happened to be trans. And nobody in that building knew the difference, including me. I needed information, not just prayer. I needed someone to explain to me what I was actually facing."

Why This Book, and Why Now

We are living in a moment when the intersection of gender, sexuality, and secrecy has become more complex than at any other point in human history. The internet has made it possible for men to explore attractions they might have previously buried entirely. Social media has made trans women, femboys, and drag queens more visible, and more accessible, than ever before. Dating apps have created entire ecosystems designed to connect men with feminine-presenting individuals, operating in complete secrecy from the women these men go home to.

And yet, the resources available to women who discover their partner's involvement in these spaces are virtually nonexistent. When J. L. King wrote his book in 2004, there were no iPhones, no Instagram, no Tinder, and the trans community's visibility was a fraction of what it is today. The conversation he started was groundbreaking for it's time, but it was incomplete. And the cultural conversation has barely moved forward since.

This book picks up where that conversation stalled. It's written for you: the woman who needs more than a bumper sticker answer. The woman who needs to understand the psychology, the patterns, the warning signs, the emotional dynamics, the health implications, and the decision-making process that comes after discovery. It's written for the woman who looked at the evidence and thought, "This isn't what I was told the down low looks like," and deserves someone to say, "You're right. It's not."

A Final Story: The Woman Who Wrote Her Own Ending

Brenda Stone Browder was J. L. King's ex-wife: the woman who was blindsided on national television when her husband chose to reveal their most private pain to Oprah Winfrey's audience without even giving her the book to read beforehand. For years after that episode aired, Brenda was defined by her husband's story. She was "the DL man's wife." She was a cautionary tale.

But Brenda refused to stay in that narrative. She wrote her own book. She became a minister. She became an advocate for women in similar situations. And she said something in interviews that I think belongs in the opening chapter of any honest book about the down low: the worst part wasn't the cheating. The worst part was not understanding what she was dealing with. The worst part was the confusion.

That confusion is what this book intends to clear up. Not by telling you what to feel or what to do, those are your choices, and every chapter that follows will give you the information you need to make them wisely; but by telling you the truth about what you're facing. The complete truth. Including the parts that nobody else has been willing to say out loud.

Because the down low is not a monolith. It's not one thing. And you deserve to know the difference.

In the chapters that follow, we're going to go deep. We'll explore the psychology behind attraction to feminine-presenting individuals. We'll compare the behavioral patterns of different types of DL men side by side. We'll examine how the hair, the nails, the body, the aesthetic, the entire investment in feminine presentation, functions as the key to this particular form of attraction. We'll hear from trans women and femboys about what it's like to be the other person in these hidden relationships. We'll address the health implications honestly and without judgment. And ultimately, we'll help you decide what to do with everything you've learned.

But before we go any further, I want you to take a breath. If you're reading this book because your world has recently been turned upside down, I need you to hear this: you are not alone. You are not stupid for not knowing. You are not less of a woman because of what he did. And whatever you decide to do next, stay, leave, or find some third path nobody's thought of yet, you are going to be okay.

Now turn the page. We've got work to do.

CHAPTER TWO

The Feminine Mystique: Understanding Attraction to Trans Women, Femboys, and Drag Queens

Let me tell you something that most people in our community already know but nobody wants to say out loud: the man who is attracted to a trans woman with a twenty-eight-inch lace front, a beat face, nails done, body smooth as silk, and a dress that's hugging every curve: that man is not looking at a man. I don't care what his birth certificate says. I don't care what your pastor says. I don't care what your mama says when you call her crying at two in the morning. That man's eyes, his brain, his body, everything in him is responding to femininity. And until we get honest about that, we're going to keep having the wrong conversation.

Now, I know that's a bold way to open a chapter. And I know some of y'all just tensed up reading it. Good. Stay with me. Because this chapter is about understanding what's actually happening inside the mind and body of a man who is attracted to trans women, femboys, and drag queens who present as feminine. Not what we assume is happening. Not what the church told us is happening. Not what Twitter debates tell us is happening. What the science, the psychology, and the lived experiences of real people actually reveal.

As someone in the LGBTQIA community, I've had a front-row seat to this conversation for years. I've watched trans women I know and love navigate relationships with men who adore them in private and deny them in public. I've sat with femboys who told me about the DMs flooding their inbox from men with wedding rings in their profile pictures. I've heard drag queens talk about the men who wait for them after the show, not to get an autograph, but to get a phone number. And through all of it, I've watched our broader culture try to shove these experiences into a box labeled "gay" when the reality is so much more complicated than that.

This chapter is for the women who need to understand what that complication actually looks like. And it starts with a question that seems simple but isn't: What is attraction, really?

What Is Attraction, Really?

We throw the word "attraction" around like it's the simplest thing in the world. He's attracted to women. She's attracted to men. Simple. Clean. Neat little boxes. But if you've ever been attracted to someone you couldn't explain, someone who wasn't your usual type, someone who surprised you, someone who made you feel something unexpected, then you already know that attraction is anything but simple.

Here's what the science tells us about how attraction actually works in the human brain: it's not a single switch that flips on or off. It's more like a symphony, dozens of instruments playing at once, some louder than others, and the overall melody changes depending on who's conducting. There are visual cues: what someone looks like, how they carry themselves, the shape of their body, their facial features. There are olfactory cues: pheromones, scent, the chemistry that happens below conscious awareness. There are behavioral cues: how someone moves, talks, laughs, the energy they give off. And there are psychological cues: what someone represents to you, the narrative you build around them, the way they make you feel about yourself.

For most heterosexual men, the loudest instruments in this symphony are the visual cues associated with femininity. And I'm not talking about some abstract, philosophical idea of femininity. I'm talking about the concrete, tangible, see-it-with-your-eyes markers that the male brain has evolved to respond to: curves, soft skin, long hair, full lips, a particular hip-to-waist ratio, a certain way of moving through space. These are the signals that trigger the attraction response in most men, and they do it fast, in milliseconds, before the conscious mind even has time to form an opinion.

Now here's the critical question this chapter is asking: When a man's brain encounters those visual cues on a person who is transgender, on a femboy, or on a drag queen who has invested in creating a convincing feminine presentation, does his brain respond differently than it would to a cisgender woman? And the answer, according to the best available research, is: not as differently as you'd think.

Malik's Story

Malik is a thirty-six-year-old electrician in Baltimore. Married for eleven years. Three kids. Active in his church. Coaches his son's basketball team. If you saw Malik at a cookout, you'd see a typical Black man living a typical Black life: the kind of brother your auntie would brag about at Thanksgiving.

But Malik has a secret that has been eating him alive for almost eight years. When he was twenty-eight, he encountered a trans woman at a gas station. She was getting into the car in front of his, and something about her stopped him cold. Long hair, fitted jeans, a cropped jacket, and a walk that Malik describes as "the kind of feminine that takes your breath." He didn't know she was trans at first. He just thought she was a beautiful woman.

Malik ended up in a conversation with her. He got her number. They texted for weeks. And when she eventually disclosed that she was transgender, Malik says something happened that he didn't expect: "It didn't change anything. I was already attracted to her. I was already feeling her. Finding out she was trans didn't make her less attractive to me. It didn't make me feel gay. It made me feel confused, because I didn't have a word for what I was."

Malik never pursued that relationship. He was too scared. But the attraction didn't go away. Over the next several years, he found himself drawn to trans women and femboys on social media, then on dating apps, and eventually into encounters that his wife knows nothing about. "If you put a regular man in front of me, muscles, beard, deep voice, I feel nothing," Malik told me. "Nothing. But put a trans woman in front of me who looks like she just stepped off a runway? My body reacts the exact same way it reacts to my wife. Because to me, she IS a woman. That's what my eyes see. That's what my body responds to."

The Science of Femininity-Based Attraction

Malik's experience isn't just an anecdote. It aligns with a growing body of scientific research that has fundamentally challenged how we think about male sexual orientation. And I want to walk you through this research carefully, because if you're a woman trying to understand your man, this is some of the most important information in the entire book.

In 2016, a team of researchers at Northwestern University led by Kevin J. Hsu and J. Michael Bailey published a study in the journal *Psychological Medicine* that set out to answer a straightforward question: Are men who are attracted to trans women more like straight men or more like gay men in their arousal patterns? They brought men into a laboratory, showed them erotic images of cisgender women, cisgender men, and trans women, and measured their physical arousal responses using genital sensors that don't lie.

The results were striking. Men who were attracted to trans women showed arousal patterns that were significantly more similar to heterosexual men than to gay men. They responded strongly to images of cisgender women. They responded strongly to images of trans women. And their responses to images of masculine-presenting men? Minimal. Almost flat. Essentially the same as what you'd see in a straight man who has no interest in men whatsoever.

The researchers concluded that this attraction pattern, which they called gynandromorphophilia, or GAMP, is best understood as a variant of heterosexual attraction rather than as a form of homosexuality. Let me say that in plain English: the men who are attracted to trans women are, by the measurement of their own bodies, responding to femininity. Not to maleness. Not to masculinity. To femininity.

A follow-up study published in 2017 in the Archives of Sexual Behavior surveyed 314 men with this attraction pattern and compared them to 211 heterosexual men who were not attracted to trans women. The men attracted to trans women reported much higher levels of attraction to women than to men. They were, on average, equally attracted to cisgender women and trans women. And critically, they did not identify as gay. Most identified as heterosexual or used terms like "straight with a twist" or "heteroflexible."

Now, I'm not a scientist. I'm a community member who reads the research and talks to real people. But when the science and the lived experience line up this closely, when the data says these men's bodies respond to femininity and the men themselves say the exact same thing, that's worth paying attention to. Especially if you're a woman who discovered your man's attraction and has been told the only possible explanation is that he's gay.

Beyond the Kinsey Scale: Why Our Old Maps Don't Work Here

Most of us, whether we know it consciously or not, understand sexuality through a model that's over seventy-five years old. In 1948, Alfred Kinsey published his groundbreaking research showing that sexuality exists on a spectrum rather than as an either-or binary. His scale ran from zero, meaning exclusively heterosexual, to six, meaning exclusively homosexual, with everything in between representing varying degrees of bisexuality. For it's time, this was revolutionary. It told America that the world wasn't just sheep and goats: that most people fall somewhere in the middle.

But here's the problem: the Kinsey scale measures attraction along a single axis, men on one end, women on the other. It assumes that if you're more attracted to one sex, you're necessarily less attracted to the other. And it has absolutely no way to account for what happens when a person is attracted to femininity itself, regardless of the biological sex of the person presenting it.

Recent scholars have pointed out that the Kinsey scale conflates two separate things: attraction to men and attraction to women. Research published in the Proceedings of the National Academy of Sciences in 2020 demonstrated that these are actually independent constructs, meaning a person's level of attraction to women doesn't necessarily tell you anything about their level of attraction to men, and vice versa. This matters enormously for the conversation we're having, because the men in this book, men attracted to trans women, femboys, and feminine-presenting drag queens, break the Kinsey model entirely.

Think about it: a man who is powerfully attracted to cisgender women AND equally attracted to trans women, but who has zero interest in masculine-presenting men, where does he fall on the Kinsey scale? He's not a zero, because he's attracted to someone who was assigned male at birth. But he's not a three or a four either, because he has no attraction to masculinity. The scale literally can't categorize him. And that failure of categorization is part of what has kept this conversation stuck for twenty years.

What we need instead is a model that separates sexual orientation from gender presentation attraction. A model that says: this man's orientation is toward femininity, full stop. His brain, his body, his desire all light up in the presence of femininity, whether that femininity is expressed by a cisgender woman, a trans woman, a femboy in a silk dress and stilettos, or a drag queen who has beat her face to the gods. And the absence of femininity, a masculine-presenting person of any biological sex, leaves him cold.

I know that's a paradigm shift for a lot of readers. I know it's easier to stick with the old boxes. But those old boxes are the reason women like you have been confused, and I'm not here to keep you comfortable. I'm here to give you the truth.

Crystal's Story

Crystal is a trans woman in her late twenties who lives in Houston. She's what many in the community would call "fish": a term used to describe a trans woman whose feminine presentation is so convincing that most people would never clock her as trans. Crystal has had breast augmentation, maintains a rigorous beauty routine, wears custom wigs that cost as much as some people's rent, and carries herself with a quiet, effortless femininity that turns heads.

Crystal has dated DL men almost exclusively since she transitioned at twenty. And she has strong opinions about the conversation this book is having. "These men are not gay," she told me bluntly. "I've dated gay men. I know what that energy feels like. The men who pursue me don't have that energy. They open my car door. They call me 'baby.' They want to take me to nice restaurants. They are attracted to me because I am a woman to them. They treat me the exact same way they treat cisgender women, because that's what they see when they look at me."

But Crystal is also clear-eyed about the pain this dynamic creates. "They love me in private," she said. "But they'll never claim me in public. I'm the one they text at midnight, not the one they bring to the company Christmas party. And every single one of them has a woman at home who has no idea I exist. That's the part that hurts. Not for me, I know what I signed up for. But for her. Because she's being lied to, and she deserves to know."

I asked Crystal what she would want to say to the wives and girlfriends. She paused for a long time. Then: "Your man's attraction to me isn't about you not being enough. I look the way I look because I've spent years and thousands of dollars to look this way. He's not choosing me over you. He's choosing me in addition to you. And that's a conversation y'all need to have with each other, not one that should happen behind closed doors while both of us are being lied to."

The Hair, the Nails, the Skin: Understanding the Visual Trigger

Let's talk about what actually activates this attraction, because it's not abstract. It's concrete. It's visual. And it's rooted in specific markers of femininity that trans women, femboys, and drag queens invest enormous time, energy, and money to achieve.

When men in these studies and in my own conversations describe what attracts them, they consistently point to the same things: long hair; and not just any hair, but styled, maintained, feminine hair, whether that's a lace front wig, a sew-in, or natural hair styled in a soft, flowing way. Smooth, hair-free skin on the body, face, and legs. Manicured nails, acrylics, gel sets, French tips, the kind of nail work that says "I invest in my femininity." Makeup applied with skill, contour, highlight, lashes, the full beat. Clothing that emphasizes the feminine form, bodycon dresses, heels, fitted jeans. And a general aura of softness, in voice, in movement, in energy.

Now, if you're a woman reading this list, you're probably thinking: "That's the same stuff that attracts men to me." And you're right. That's exactly the point. The visual cues that trigger attraction in these men are the same visual cues that trigger attraction in every heterosexual man. The difference is that these men respond to those cues regardless of the biological sex of the person displaying them. A cisgender woman in a red dress with a twenty-two-inch wig and a full face of makeup? Attractive. A trans woman in the same outfit, with the same energy? Equally attractive. A femboy who has achieved a smooth, soft, feminine look through careful grooming and styling? Attractive.

There's a term that gets used in the trans community, "passing." It refers to how convincingly a trans person presents as their identified gender. And while the concept of passing is debated within the LGBTQIA community, some argue it reinforces cisnormative standards, it is undeniably relevant to this conversation. The research from Northwestern showed a correlation between the degree of feminine presentation and the intensity of attraction: the more feminine the presentation, the stronger the response. This isn't about judging trans women or femboys on a scale of "how female do they look." It's about understanding the mechanics of how attraction works in these men's brains.

And here's where I want to get really real with you, sis. The trans women and femboys who are involved with DL men aren't doing this by accident. Many of them, not all, but many, have invested staggering amounts of money into their appearance. We're talking hormone therapy, surgical procedures, custom wigs that run four hundred to a thousand dollars each, monthly nail appointments, skincare regimens, laser hair removal or regular waxing, and wardrobes that rival any Instagram influencer. The feminine presentation that attracts these DL men is not effortless. It is a craft. And the result is a person who, walking down the street, would be seen by ninety-nine percent of people as simply a beautiful woman.

For the woman who has discovered that her man is attracted to someone like this, it creates a particularly agonizing form of cognitive dissonance. You expected to find out your man was interested in men. Instead, you're looking at photos of someone who looks like a woman; and often, a woman who looks better than most women you know, because she has invested more in her appearance than most cisgender women ever will. You don't know whether to be angry, confused, intimidated, or all three at once.

Dee's Story

Dee is twenty-four and identifies as a femboy. Born and raised in Detroit, Dee grew up in a house where masculinity was the only acceptable way to present. But from the time Dee was a teenager, there was a pull toward femininity that couldn't be denied, nail polish worn only behind closed doors, a fascination with YouTube makeup tutorials, and a deep admiration for the trans women and feminine gay men who seemed to live freely in a way Dee only dreamed of.

By twenty, Dee had begun presenting publicly as feminine. Long nails. Styled hair. Smooth, shaved skin. Fitted, feminine clothing. Not a full transition, Dee doesn't identify as a woman, but an embrace of femininity that is unmistakable. On social media, Dee's photos could easily be mistaken for those of a cisgender woman. The DMs from DL men started almost immediately.

"The first thing they always say," Dee told me, "is 'You're so pretty.' Not 'You're so handsome.' Not 'You're so fine, bro.' They call me pretty. Beautiful. Gorgeous. They talk to me the way they talk to women, because that's what they see. And most of them, when I tell them I'm not a woman, they say, 'I don't care what you identify as, to me you're beautiful and that's what I'm attracted to.'"

Dee has been involved with several DL men, all of whom were in relationships with women. One of them, a thirty-one-year-old financial advisor, took Dee on actual dates, restaurants, movies, shopping trips, in cities far enough away from home that they wouldn't be recognized. "He treated me like a girlfriend," Dee said. "He opened doors, he paid for everything, he told me I was the most feminine person he'd ever been with. And when I asked him if he was gay, he looked genuinely insulted. He said, 'Bro, I'm attracted to femininity. You're the most feminine person I know. How does that make me gay?'"

It's a fair question. And it's the question this entire chapter is trying to help you sit with.

This Is Not the Same as Homosexuality: Here's Why That Matters

I want to take a moment here to speak directly, from one community member to the women reading this. I am a member of the LGBTQIA community. I love and support gay men, bisexual men, trans women, trans men, nonbinary people, and every letter in that alphabet. This is not a book that demonizes any sexual orientation or gender identity. Being gay is not a disease, a curse, or a character flaw, and any suggestion otherwise is something I reject entirely.

But honesty requires me to say this: the attraction pattern we're discussing in this chapter is not homosexuality. And pretending it is, for the sake of simplicity, for the sake of having a familiar label to slap on it, for the sake of giving you a culturally scripted response, is a disservice to you, to the men involved, and to the LGBTQIA community itself.

Here's why the distinction matters:

Homosexuality, at its core, is attraction to the same sex and gender. A gay man is attracted to men, to masculinity, to the male body, to the male form. When a gay man watches adult content, he's watching men. When a gay man fantasizes, he's fantasizing about men. When a gay man falls in love, he falls in love with a man who presents as a man. That is his orientation, and there is absolutely nothing wrong with it.

The men we're discussing are experiencing something different. When they consume adult content; and as we discussed in Chapter 1, the data shows they're consuming trans and femboy content at staggering rates: they are not watching masculine men. They are watching feminine-presenting individuals. When they fantasize, the object of their fantasy looks like a woman. When they pursue someone on a dating app, the person they're swiping right on looks like a woman. The entire architecture of their desire is oriented toward femininity.

Does this make them "straight" in the traditional sense? Not exactly. Does it make them gay? The science says no. Does it make them bisexual? Maybe, by some definitions. But most of these men don't feel like any of those labels fit, because none of those labels were designed to describe what they're experiencing. They exist in a space that our language hasn't caught up to yet. And living in that unnamed space, in a culture that demands you pick a lane, is part of what drives the secrecy.

James's Story

James is forty-four and lives in Charlotte, North Carolina. He's a divorced father of two. His ex-wife, Sharon, left him three years ago after discovering his involvement with a trans woman named Melody. James agreed to share his story because, as he put it, "maybe if somebody had explained this to Sharon before she found out, we could have had a different conversation."

James grew up in a strictly religious household in rural South Carolina. He played football, dated girls, lost his virginity at sixteen to his high school girlfriend, and never once experienced attraction to a man. "I need you to understand," he said, leaning forward. "I have never in my life looked at a man and felt anything. Not in the locker room. Not in the military. Not anywhere. Men do nothing for me."

His attraction to trans women began when he was stationed overseas in his twenties. He encountered a group of trans women at a nightclub in Thailand: a country with a long, visible tradition of trans feminine individuals. He was initially unaware they were trans. When he found out, he expected to feel repulsed. He didn't. "They were the most beautiful, feminine women I'd ever seen," he said. "And my body didn't care about their biology. My body cared about what it saw."

James spent years compartmentalizing this attraction. He married Sharon, had children, and built what looked like a conventional life. But the attraction to trans women never went away. He describes it as being hardwired, as fundamental and unchangeable as his attraction to cisgender women. "I tried to pray it away," he said. "I tried to ignore it. I tried to tell myself it was just a phase, a curiosity. It's not. It's who I am. I am a man who is attracted to femininity in all it's forms. And I'm tired of pretending that makes me something I'm not."

When I asked James what he wished Sharon had known, he said: "I wish she knew that my attraction to Melody had nothing to do with not wanting her. I wanted them both. Not because I'm greedy, but because they both represented what I'm attracted to: beautiful, feminine women. The only difference was that one of them was trans. And in my mind, in my heart, that wasn't a disqualifying difference."

The Drag Queen Factor: When Performance Becomes Desire

We've talked about trans women, who live as women full-time. We've talked about femboys, who embrace a feminine aesthetic as a consistent part of their identity. But there's a third group that deserves its own discussion in this chapter: drag queens, specifically, the ones whose feminine transformation is so compelling that it generates genuine sexual and romantic attraction from men.

Now, before the drag community comes for me, let me be clear: most drag is art, performance, and entertainment. Most drag queens are fully aware that their feminine presentation is a costume: a character they put on for the stage. And most men who appreciate drag are appreciating the artistry, not experiencing sexual attraction. This is not about those men.

This is about the subset of men, a subset that is larger than most people realize, who see a drag queen in full glam and experience genuine, visceral, physiological attraction. The kind of attraction that makes them seek out the queen after the show. The kind that makes them follow her on social media. The kind that makes them DM her not about booking her for an event, but about taking her to dinner. I know this happens because I've seen it happen. I've been in the rooms, the clubs, the spaces where this plays out. And the queens will tell you: it's more common than anyone admits.

What's happening here is an extension of the same femininity-based attraction we've been discussing. When a drag queen transforms, when the wig goes on, the makeup is flawless, the body is padded and contoured, the nails are done, the outfit is snatched: the visual result can be indistinguishable from a cisgender woman to the untrained eye. And for men whose attraction is triggered by femininity, that visual result is enough. Their brain doesn't say, "Wait, that's a man in a costume." Their brain says, "That's a beautiful woman." And once the attraction fires, it's not easily turned off by intellectual knowledge of what's underneath the transformation.

For women, this adds yet another layer of complexity. Your man might not be pursuing someone who lives as a woman full-time. He might be attracted to someone who is a man by day and a stunning woman by night. And if that sounds confusing, imagine how it feels for him, attracted to someone whose femininity is temporary, performative, and yet absolutely real in the moment it's happening.

Tony's Story

Tony is a fifty-one-year-old bar owner in Washington, D. C. His establishment hosts drag shows every Friday and Saturday night. Tony's wife, Linda, thinks the drag shows are purely a business decision, good for revenue, good for the community. What Linda doesn't know is that Tony's relationship with drag performance is deeply personal.

"The first time I was attracted to a drag queen, I was maybe twenty-five," Tony told me. "I went to a show with some friends as a joke. We were all laughing, having a good time. And then this queen came out on stage and I swear to you, I forgot she was a man. Everything about her was woman. The way she moved, the way she looked, the confidence. I couldn't stop staring. My boys were laughing and I was sitting there with my heart racing."

Tony's attraction didn't stop after that night. He began seeking out drag shows, and eventually, he began pursuing relationships with drag queens who maintained a particularly feminine presentation. One queen, who performed under the name "Velvet," became Tony's first full emotional affair. They dated for nearly a year, dinners, weeknight visits, regular phone calls. Velvet performed in drag on weekends but maintained a more androgynous look during the week. Tony admits he was more attracted to Velvet in full drag than out of it. "In drag, she was my fantasy," he said. "Out of drag, I cared about her, him, as a person. But the attraction was strongest when the femininity was at its peak."

Tony's wife still doesn't know. And Tony is deeply conflicted. "I'm not gay," he insists. "I've been with Linda for twenty-three years and I'm attracted to her. I love my wife. But I'm also attracted to something she can't give me, and I don't even know what to call it."

What the LGBTQIA Community Says, And Doesn't Say

I'd be lying if I told you the LGBTQIA community has this figured out. We don't. The truth is, there are heated debates within our own community about men who pursue trans women and femboys, and those debates mirror much of the confusion happening in the broader culture.

Some members of the gay community argue that these men are simply in denial about being gay or bisexual: that attraction to anyone who was assigned male at birth makes you, at minimum, bisexual, full stop. I understand that perspective. It comes from a place of wanting clarity, and from a frustration with men who benefit from heterosexual privilege while secretly engaging in what could be seen as same-sex contact.

Many trans women, on the other hand, take strong issue with that framing. They argue, and I think they make a compelling point, that calling a man gay for being attracted to them invalidates their womanhood. If a trans woman is a woman, then a man who is attracted to her is attracted to a woman. Calling him gay contradicts the very recognition of trans identity that the LGBTQIA movement has fought so hard to establish.

And then there are those in the community who simply say: labels are less important than honesty. A man can be attracted to whoever he's attracted to: the problem isn't the attraction, it's the lying. If he were honest with the woman at home about who he is and what he desires, we wouldn't need a book like this. The secrecy is the issue, not the sexuality.

I fall closest to that last camp. I've watched this debate go around in circles for years, and I've come to believe that the most loving, most honest, and most productive approach is to stop arguing about what to call these men and start focusing on what to do about the deception. The women at home deserve honesty. The trans women and femboys being treated as secrets deserve dignity. And the men hiding in the shadows deserve the chance to live in the light, even if the light is terrifying.

But none of that can happen as long as we're stuck in a conversation that insists on cramming every human experience into boxes that were built for a simpler time. And that's why this chapter matters. It's not trying to convince you of a label. It's trying to show you a reality. What you do with that reality is entirely up to you.

What This Means for You

If you've made it this far in the chapter, you might be feeling a swirl of emotions. Maybe you're nodding because this finally explains something that never made sense before. Maybe you're angry because you feel like I'm making excuses for men's dishonesty. Maybe you're grieving because you realize your man's attraction isn't something that can be prayed away, therapied away, or punished away, it's a fundamental part of how his brain processes desire.

All of those feelings are valid. And I want to sit with you in them for a moment before we close this chapter.

Understanding the psychology and biology behind your man's attraction does not mean you have to accept the lying, the sneaking, or the betrayal. Those are choices he made. He chose to hide. He chose to build a secret life. He chose to put you at risk, emotionally and potentially physically. Nothing in this chapter excuses those choices. A man can have a complex attraction pattern and still be honest with the woman he claims to love. The attraction is not the sin. The secrecy is.

But understanding the nature of the attraction does help you in several critical ways. First, it helps you stop blaming yourself. His attraction to a trans woman or a femboy has nothing to do with you not being feminine enough, sexy enough, or good enough. He is attracted to femininity in a broader range of expressions than most men. That's about him, not you. Second, it helps you stop expecting a simple fix. If you think your man is just a closeted gay man who needs to come out, you might assume that if he just "admits" he's gay, the problem is solved. But if his attraction is to femininity rather than to masculinity, telling him to come out as gay doesn't actually address what's happening. Third, it helps you have a more honest conversation, with him, with a therapist, and with yourself, about what the future looks like.

In the next chapter, we're going to lay out a detailed, side-by-side comparison of DL men who pursue masculine men versus DL men who pursue feminine-presenting individuals. We'll look at their behaviors, their digital footprints, their relationship patterns, and the ways their secrecy manifests differently. Because understanding the psychology is step one. Understanding the pattern is step two. And that's where the real tools for protecting yourself begin.

But before you turn the page, I want to leave you with something Crystal said that has stayed with me since our conversation. When I asked her what she thought the biggest misconception was about the men who pursue her, she said:

"Everybody wants to call them gay because it's easier. It's a word people understand. But calling them gay doesn't explain why they walked past a hundred men to get to me. It doesn't explain why they don't want a man. It doesn't explain why they treat me like a queen, pun intended, and have zero interest in anything masculine.

Calling them gay is lazy. And lazy answers hurt the women at home just as much as they hurt us."

She's right. And lazy answers are something this book refuses to provide. I've spent too many years in this community watching people get hurt because we were all too afraid to tell the full truth. Trans women getting used and discarded in secret. Women at home getting lied to by men they built their lives around. And the men themselves, trapped in a prison of shame and silence because our culture told them they had to be one thing or another, gay or straight, this or that, and they knew in their bones they were neither.

The truth is messier than the labels. It always has been. But messy doesn't mean incomprehensible. And now that you understand the psychology, now that you know what the research says, what the men themselves describe, and what the people on the other side of these secret relationships experience, you're better equipped than ninety-nine percent of women who have ever found themselves in this situation.

Hold on to that. We're just getting started. Let's keep going.

CHAPTER THREE

Two Different Worlds: DL Men Who Deal with Men vs. DL Men Who Deal with Fem-Presenting Individuals

Alright, sis. We've laid the groundwork. You understand the history. You understand the psychology. Now it's time to put the two worlds side by side so you can see, clearly, without anybody sugarcoating it, exactly how different these two types of DL behavior really are. Because the way a man who is secretly dealing with other men operates is fundamentally different from the way a man who is secretly dealing with trans women, femboys, or drag queens operates. The apps are different. The meeting places are different. The relationship dynamics are different. The emotional patterns are different. The way they rationalize what they're doing is different.

And what all of that means for you, the woman at home, is different.

I'm going to walk you through both worlds in detail. Not because I'm trying to rank one as worse than the other, betrayal is betrayal, and a lie is a lie regardless of who your man is lying with; but because understanding the specific pattern you're dealing with is the key to understanding what comes next. You can't navigate a situation you don't understand. And right now, too many women are trying to navigate their situation using a map that was drawn for somebody else's journey.

So let's draw the right map.

World One: The DL Man Who Deals with Masculine-Presenting Men

Let's start with the version of the down low that America has been talking about since 2004: the man who is secretly having sexual encounters with other men who look, dress, and present as men. This is the J. L. King model. This is what Oprah talked about. This is what your girlfriend is picturing in her mind when you tell her you think something is going on with your man. And while this version has been discussed extensively, it's worth laying out the behavioral patterns in detail because we need a clear baseline for comparison.

How He Finds Partners

The DL man who pursues masculine-presenting men typically relies on technology that is designed specifically for men seeking men. The apps of choice are platforms like Grindr, Jack'd, SCRUFF, and Adam4Adam, apps that use location-based technology to show other men in the immediate area who are available for connection. These apps are overwhelmingly populated by men seeking men, and they are designed for efficiency: profiles feature photos (often of the body, not the face), basic physical stats, and a description of what the user is looking for. The culture of these apps favors speed and anonymity. Research published in the Journal of Acquired Immune Deficiency Syndromes found that the majority of men who have sex with men who use dating apps use them specifically to find sexual partners, with many reporting that the apps facilitate encounters that happen within hours or even minutes of the initial connection.

For the DL man, these apps offer a critical feature: discretion. He can create a profile with no face picture. He can use a fake name. He can set his distance radius to avoid being seen by people who might know him. And he can delete the app entirely after each use, reinstalling it only when the urge strikes. This install-delete-reinstall cycle is one of the most common behavioral patterns among DL men who use hookup apps, and it's something women should be aware of; because it means the app may not be on his phone at any given moment, even if he's using it regularly.

Beyond apps, DL men who pursue masculine men may also find partners through more traditional channels: certain bathhouses or sex clubs in larger cities, cruising areas in parks or public spaces, and, increasingly rarely but still happening, through personal ads on websites like Craigslist (before it's personal ads were shut down) or Reddit forums. The common thread across all of these channels is that they are designed for quick, anonymous encounters between men.

What the Encounters Look Like

The encounters themselves tend to follow a specific pattern. They are usually sexual in nature with minimal emotional connection. Many DL men who pursue masculine men describe their encounters as transactional: a physical need that gets met, quickly and quietly, with no strings attached. They take place in cars, in the other person's apartment, in bathhouse facilities, or in other spaces that minimize the risk of being seen. The encounters are often short, sometimes lasting less than thirty minutes, and are followed by an immediate return to the man's "real life." There is typically no texting afterward, no follow-up, no relationship building. It's a compartmentalized behavior: the encounter exists in its own sealed box, separate from everything else in his life.

I've talked to men who operate in this space, and the language they use is telling. They describe what they do in clinical, detached terms: "getting off," "handling business," "taking care of a need."

There's very little romance in the language because there's very little romance in the behavior. This is about a physical drive, and the man has found a way to satisfy it while keeping it as far from his emotional and domestic life as possible.

How He Rationalizes It

The rationalization is almost always the same: "It's just sex. It doesn't mean anything. I'm not gay. I love my woman. This is just something I do sometimes." The DL man who pursues masculine men typically draws a hard line between sex and identity. In his mind, having sex with a man doesn't make him gay because he doesn't love men, doesn't date men, and doesn't want to build a life with a man. He sees his encounters as a behavior, not an identity. And that distinction, however fragile it might seem from the outside, is the psychological architecture that allows him to go home, kiss his wife, and sleep peacefully.

This rationalization is reinforced by the nature of the encounters themselves. Because they are quick, anonymous, and emotionless, they feel temporary. They feel like something that can be turned on and off. They feel, to the man involved, like they don't really count. And that's what makes them so dangerous for the woman at home; because in his mind, he's not really cheating. He's just doing something on the side that has nothing to do with his real life.

Reggie's Story

Reggie is forty years old, lives in Memphis, and has been married for fourteen years. He's a deacon at his church, a high school basketball coach, and by every outward measure, the epitome of traditional Black masculinity. His wife, Tameka, describes him as "the manliest man I know."

Reggie has been having sexual encounters with men since he was in college. Always masculine-presenting men. Always in secret. Always quick. He uses Grindr but never keeps it on his phone for more than a few hours at a time. He drives to the next city over, never meets anyone in Memphis. His profile has no face, no name, just his physical stats and the words "straight, discreet, DL only."

"I don't feel anything for these men," Reggie told me. "I'm not attracted to them as people. I don't want to know their names. I don't want to grab dinner. I need something physical that I can't get from Tameka, and I get it, and I go home. Is it wrong? Probably. But it's no different in my mind than watching something online. It's a physical release. That's it."

When I asked Reggie if he was gay, he became visibly agitated. "I am not gay. I have never been in love with a man. I have never wanted to hold a man's hand, take a man to dinner, introduce a man to my family. I love women. I love my wife. I just have this other thing that I deal with, and I deal with it as quietly as possible."

World Two: The DL Man Who Deals with Trans Women, Femboys, and Drag Queens

Now let's cross over into the other world: the one this book exists to illuminate. The DL man who pursues trans women, femboys, and drag queens who present as feminine. And I want you to pay close attention here, because almost everything about this pattern is different from what we just described.

How He Finds Partners

The first difference is the digital ecosystem. This man is typically not on Grindr, SCRUFF, or Jack'd, apps designed for men seeking men. He's on platforms that specifically cater to men interested in trans women and feminine-presenting individuals. Apps like Taimi, Butterfly, and My Transgender Cupid are designed for this purpose. Some men use mainstream dating apps like Tinder or Hinge but filter their preferences to include trans women. Others find their connections through social media, particularly Instagram, TikTok, and Twitter, where trans women and femboys with large followings post content that draws attention from admirers.

The way this man browses is fundamentally different from the way the first type of DL man browses. He's not looking at faceless torso pics. He's looking at full, glamorous photos of feminine-presenting individuals: selfies with lace fronts and beat faces, outfit-of-the-day posts, beauty tutorials, lifestyle content. His browsing behavior looks, for all intents and purposes, like a straight man scrolling through a beautiful woman's Instagram page. Because that's what he thinks he's doing.

Many of these men also find partners through in-person spaces that are connected to the LGBTQIA community but are distinct from the spaces used by men seeking men. Drag shows at clubs and lounges. Trans-friendly nightlife venues. Ballroom culture events, and I say this as someone who has deep roots in ballroom, where the lines between admiration and attraction get blurry in environments that celebrate femininity in all it's forms. Some men first encounter trans women or femboys at these events and find themselves drawn in by the energy, the beauty, and the unapologetic femininity on display.

What the Encounters Look Like

And this is where the two worlds diverge most dramatically. Unlike the quick, anonymous, emotionless encounters that characterize the first type of DL behavior, the relationships between DL men and trans women or femboys frequently involve genuine dating. I'm talking about dinner at a restaurant. I'm talking about weekend trips. I'm talking about hours-long phone conversations, good-morning texts, pet names, inside jokes, and the full emotional vocabulary of a romantic relationship.

These men don't just want sex. Many of them want connection. They want to be seen, known, and appreciated by someone who embodies the femininity they're drawn to. They want the experience of courting a beautiful woman; because in their eyes, that's exactly what they're doing. And the trans women and femboys in these relationships often confirm this: the dynamic mirrors a heterosexual relationship in virtually every way.

There's often a significant financial component as well. DL men in these relationships frequently provide financial support to their trans or femboy partners, paying for hair, nails, clothing, rent, phone bills, and other expenses. Some of this is genuine generosity driven by affection. Some of it is transactional, an unspoken agreement that financial support buys discretion and availability. And some of it is a combination of both. The financial dimension adds another layer of complexity for the woman at home, because unexplained spending or financial irregularities may be among the first warning signs she notices.

How He Rationalizes It

The rationalization is completely different from the first type. While the DL man who pursues masculine men says "It's just sex, it doesn't mean anything," the DL man who pursues trans women and femboys often cannot say that. Because it does mean something. He's not just satisfying a physical need, he's building a relationship with a person he's genuinely attracted to, a person he may genuinely care about.

His rationalization instead tends to center on the femininity argument: "I'm not cheating with a man. I'm attracted to women. She's a woman to me." In his mind, his behavior is more like a traditional affair than like what the world calls "being on the DL." He frames it as cheating, which is bad enough, but not as homosexual behavior. And because the person he's involved with looks, acts, and presents as a woman, that rationalization has a certain internal consistency that the first type's rationalization lacks.

I've heard men in this category say things like: "If you saw her on the street, you'd think she was a woman. If you saw us together at a restaurant, you'd think we were a regular couple. So how is this any different from a regular affair?" And honestly? From the perspective of behavior, the dating, the emotional attachment, the romantic dynamic, it isn't very different from a regular affair. Except that the "other woman" is transgender, and that single fact transforms the entire social and cultural meaning of the betrayal.

Tiffany and Leon's Story

Tiffany is a thirty-three-year-old nurse in Dallas. She discovered her fiancé Leon's secret life six months before their planned wedding. The discovery didn't come through a hookup app or a suspicious text message. It came through Venmo.

Tiffany noticed that Leon had been sending regular payments to someone named "Jasmine." Small amounts at first, fifty dollars here, a hundred there, but they had been increasing steadily. When she asked Leon about it, he said Jasmine was a coworker he was helping out. Tiffany believed him. Until she searched the name on Instagram and found Jasmine's page: a gorgeous trans woman with a significant following, who posted beauty content, outfit photos, and the occasional couple's photo with a man whose face was always cropped out or obscured by an emoji. Tiffany recognized Leon's watch in one of the photos.

"The thing that destroyed me," Tiffany said, "wasn't just that he was cheating. It was how he was cheating. This wasn't some quick thing in a parking lot. He was taking this girl out. He was buying her things. He was posting with her, well, almost posting. He had a whole relationship that looked exactly like ours. Dinner dates, weekend hangouts, matching outfits. When I confronted him, he cried. Not because he got caught. Because he said he cared about both of us and he didn't want to lose either one."

Tiffany called off the wedding. But the confusion she felt, and still feels, is the reason she gave me permission to share her story. "If he had cheated with another woman, a regular woman, I would have known how to feel. If he had cheated with a man, I would have known how to feel. But he cheated with a trans woman who looked like a supermodel, and he wasn't on a hookup app, and he was taking her to the Cheesecake Factory, and he was crying because he loves her too. I didn't have a script for that. I still don't."

The Side-by-Side: Key Differences That Matter

Let me lay out the key differences between these two patterns in plain terms, because this is the core of what women need to understand. I'm not putting these in a chart because this book is a conversation, not a textbook. But I want you to pay attention to each one, because they have direct implications for what you're dealing with and how you should think about it.

Emotional Investment

The DL man who deals with masculine men typically has low emotional investment in his encounters. They are sexual, not romantic. He doesn't know or care about his partner's life outside the encounter. The DL man who deals with trans women and femboys, by contrast, often has high emotional investment. He dates. He texts. He shares. He cares. For the woman at home, this means the threat is not just sexual, it's emotional. You may not just be competing with a physical act. You may be competing with an entire parallel relationship.

Duration and Frequency

Encounters with masculine men tend to be infrequent and brief, driven by impulse rather than schedule. Relationships with trans women and femboys tend to be ongoing, regular, and structured, involving planned dates, consistent communication, and a rhythm that mirrors a committed relationship. This means the amount of time, energy, and attention being diverted from your relationship may be significantly greater with the second type.

Financial Footprint

Quick, anonymous hookups with masculine men typically leave a minimal financial footprint. Maybe a hotel room occasionally. Maybe some gas money for the drive. But relationships with trans women and femboys often involve significant financial outflows: gifts, dinners, Venmo payments, CashApp transfers, rent contributions, beauty-related expenses. If your man's finances don't add up, and the money trail leads to regular payments to a single person, you may be looking at the second type of DL behavior.

Digital Footprint

The digital footprint is different in nature, not just in degree. The man on Grindr may have a faceless profile that exists for hours at a time before being deleted. The man pursuing trans women may have a full-fledged burner Instagram account where he follows hundreds of trans influencers, a dating profile on a trans-specific app with curated photos and a detailed bio, and a text message history that reads like a love letter collection. He may also have a separate phone entirely: a burner phone that his wife doesn't know about. The digital trail of an emotional, ongoing relationship is inevitably deeper and wider than the digital trail of anonymous hookups.

Risk of Discovery

Paradoxically, the man involved in emotional relationships with trans women and femboys may be at higher risk of being discovered, precisely because the relationship is more complex. More communication means more opportunities for a text to pop up at the wrong time. More dates means more chances of being seen. More financial transactions means a longer paper trail. More emotional investment means the other person, the trans woman or femboy, has more leverage and more reason to feel aggrieved if the man doesn't deliver on his promises. Multiple DL men have been exposed not because their wife caught them, but because the person on the other side got tired of being a secret and took matters into their own hands.

Identity and Self-Perception

This is perhaps the most profound difference. The DL man who pursues masculine men, at some level, knows that what he's doing involves same-sex contact. He may not call himself gay, he may reject every label, but he knows that when he's with another man, he's with a man. The DL man who pursues trans women and femboys often genuinely does not perceive his behavior as same-sex contact at all. He sees a woman. He feels heterosexual. He experiences the relationship as a straight man experiencing a straight relationship. And that self-perception, however you might personally feel about it's accuracy, profoundly shapes how he relates to his behavior, how much shame he carries, and how he might respond if confronted.

The Shame Signature

Both types of DL men carry shame, but the shame manifests differently. The DL man who pursues masculine men carries the shame of homosexuality in a culture that punishes it, especially in the Black community, where, as we discussed in Chapter 1, the intersection of religion, masculinity expectations, and community standing creates enormous pressure. His shame sounds like: "I'm not a real man. Something is wrong with me. If people found out, they'd never look at me the same."

The DL man who pursues trans women and femboys carries a different flavor of shame, one that is, in some ways, even more isolating. His shame isn't just about homosexuality, because he doesn't see himself as homosexual. His shame is about the taboo: the cultural judgment that says attraction to trans women is freakish, deviant, or something to be mocked. He's seen the jokes on social media. He's heard the way men talk about other men who "got caught" with a trans woman. He knows that in many circles, being exposed as attracted to trans women is treated as more humiliating than being exposed as gay. Because at least being gay is now something the culture has a framework for. Being attracted to trans women? That's still treated as the punchline of a joke. And nobody wants to be the punchline.

How He Responds When Caught

Finally, and this is crucial for women preparing for a confrontation: these two types of DL men tend to respond very differently when the truth comes out. The DL man who pursues masculine men often responds with denial, deflection, and anger. He minimizes what happened. He calls it a one-time thing. He may become hostile or attempt to turn the situation around on the woman, questioning her loyalty, her snooping, anything to take the spotlight off his behavior. His primary instinct is to seal the trapdoor shut and pretend it was never there.

The DL man who pursues trans women and femboys is more likely to respond with an emotional collapse. Tears, confession, even relief. Because he has been carrying the weight of a full parallel relationship, not just a series of brief encounters, and the weight of that deception is enormous. Many women report that when they confronted their man about his involvement with a trans woman, the man didn't fight. He cried. He said he was tired of hiding. He said he was sorry. And in some cases, he said something that the woman found even more devastating than anger: he said he was in love.

Monique's Story

Monique is forty-seven and lives in Atlanta. She was married to her husband, Derek, for twenty-two years before discovering his involvement with trans women. What makes Monique's story worth telling is that she had already been through a DL discovery once before, with a previous boyfriend who had been secretly sleeping with men.

"The first time, with my ex, it was classic DL," Monique told me. "Hookup apps, anonymous stuff, no names, no faces. When I found out, I was devastated, but I understood what I was dealing with. He was a closeted gay man. It was painful, but it was clear."

With Derek, the experience was completely different. "Derek wasn't on Grindr. He wasn't in bathhouses. He was on Instagram, following trans models. He was on a dating app I'd never heard of, talking to trans women like they were his girlfriends. He had one trans woman he'd been seeing for almost three years: they had a whole thing. Dates, gifts, trips. When I found the messages, it didn't even sound like what I'd experienced before. It sounded like he had a second wife."

Monique's comparison is invaluable because she experienced both types of DL behavior firsthand. "With my ex, I could categorize it. It was gay. It was clear. I was hurt, but I could process it. With Derek, I was spinning. I didn't know what to call it. I didn't know who to tell. I couldn't even explain it to my own mother without her getting confused. She kept saying, 'So he's gay?' And I kept saying, 'I don't think so, but I don't know what he is.' That confusion, that not-knowing, was almost worse than the betrayal itself."

How the Secrecy Is Built: Two Different Architectures of Deception

One of the things I want women to understand is that these two types of DL men build fundamentally different structures of secrecy. And recognizing the structure can help you understand what you're dealing with even before you have all the evidence.

The DL man who pursues masculine men builds what I call a "trapdoor" system of secrecy. His entire secret life is designed to disappear at a moment's notice. The app gets deleted. The anonymous profile vanishes. The encounter leaves no physical evidence. There are no gifts to explain, no photos to find, no ongoing communication to intercept. If his wife suddenly picks up his phone, there's nothing there. He has built a trapdoor: he steps through it, does what he does, steps back through, and the door closes behind him as if it never existed. This kind of secrecy is extraordinarily difficult to detect because it leaves such a small footprint.

The DL man who pursues trans women and femboys builds something different, what I call a "second life" system of secrecy. Because his involvement is ongoing, emotional, and relational, he can't just open and close a trapdoor. He has to maintain an entire parallel existence. That means a second phone, or at minimum, a heavily protected section of his primary phone. It means a second set of social media accounts. It means regular blocks of time that have to be accounted for, lies about working late, going to the gym, meeting a friend, running errands that take suspiciously long. It means financial flows that have to be hidden or disguised. It means emotional energy that has to be divided between two relationships, and the inevitable fatigue that comes from maintaining two complete emotional lives simultaneously.

The "second life" architecture is inherently more fragile than the "trapdoor" system. There are more moving parts, more potential points of failure, more opportunities for the truth to leak out. And this is why, in my experience, women who are in relationships with the second type of DL man tend to discover the truth through accumulation: a series of small inconsistencies that eventually add up to an undeniable picture, rather than through a single dramatic discovery.

Shonda's Story

Shonda is thirty-nine and lives in Philadelphia. She's a high school principal, sharp, observant, and detail-oriented by nature. Which made it even more painful when she realized that her husband, Kevin, had been maintaining a parallel relationship with a trans woman named Sasha for over four years without her knowing.

The discovery didn't come all at once. It came in pieces. First, Shonda noticed that Kevin had started going to the gym at unusual hours, late at night, after the kids were in bed. Then she noticed that he had started buying a particular brand of cologne that she hadn't picked out. Then there were the frequent "work dinners" that never showed up on the credit card statement; because he was paying cash. Then a Venmo notification on his phone that popped up while he was in the shower: "Sasha sent a heart emoji for your payment."

When Shonda finally confronted Kevin, she had already assembled an entire timeline. She had screenshots, transaction records, and the Instagram page of a stunningly beautiful woman named Sasha who lived twenty minutes away. "The thing that haunts me," Shonda told me, "is how normal their relationship looked. I read their text messages. It was 'Good morning beautiful.' It was 'I miss you.' It was 'What should we eat tonight?' It was exactly how he used to talk to me when we were dating. He had recreated our entire courtship with someone else."

Kevin's response when confronted was not to deny, but to break down. He told Shonda that he had been fighting this attraction for his entire adult life. That he loved Shonda completely. That his feelings for Sasha didn't diminish his feelings for his wife. That he saw both of them as women he loved, and that he had been drowning in the impossibility of reconciling those two truths. "He wasn't angry that I found out," Shonda said. "He was relieved. And somehow, his relief made me angrier than anything else. Because he had been carrying this burden for four years, and his relief came at the cost of my entire world falling apart."

The Social Ecosystem: Who Knows and Who Doesn't

Another critical difference between these two worlds is who else knows about the man's secret life; and this matters because it affects how the truth eventually comes out and what your support system looks like when it does.

The DL man who pursues masculine men typically operates in complete isolation. Nobody in his regular life knows. Not his best friend. Not his brother. Not his barber. The encounters are with strangers who have no connection to his real life, and both parties are equally invested in secrecy. This means that when a woman discovers her man's DL behavior in this category, it's usually through direct evidence: a forgotten app on his phone, a message he didn't delete, an STI that can't be explained. The discovery comes from inside the man's digital or physical world.

The DL man who pursues trans women and femboys, however, exists within a social ecosystem that is much harder to keep contained. The trans woman or femboy he's involved with has friends, a social media presence, and a community. In the LGBTQIA spaces I move through, everybody talks. Trust me when I tell you: if a well-known DL man is dating a trans woman in a city with any kind of queer community, people know. The trans woman's friends know. The people at the ballroom know. The people at the club know. The information exists in a network that the man's wife has no access to; but that doesn't mean it's locked away forever.

This is why some women discover their man's involvement not through his phone or his finances, but through a third party. A friend of a friend who recognized him at a trans-friendly venue. A coworker who saw his car parked outside an apartment in a neighborhood he has no reason to be in. Or, most devastatingly, the trans woman or femboy themselves, who, tired of being kept a secret, decides to reach out to the wife or girlfriend directly. This last scenario is more common than you'd think, and it's one of the things that makes the second type of DL behavior so volatile for everyone involved.

What This Means for the Woman at Home

I want to speak directly to you now, because if you've recognized your situation in either of these descriptions, you're probably in pain. And you deserve to hear something honest about what each of these patterns means for your life going forward.

If your man falls into the first category, secretly pursuing masculine-presenting men, you are dealing with a man who has some form of same-sex attraction that he has been hiding. The path forward for this type of situation, while painful, is at least culturally mapped. There are support groups, therapists who specialize in this dynamic, and a body of literature that addresses what happens when a woman discovers her husband is attracted to men. You have resources. The conversation has been happening for twenty years.

If your man falls into the second category, secretly pursuing trans women, femboys, or drag queens who present as feminine, you are dealing with a more complex situation that fewer resources address. The emotional investment is likely deeper. The relationship is likely more entangled. And the identity questions are harder to resolve, because your man may genuinely not see himself as gay or even bisexual, and the science, as we discussed in the previous chapters, suggests he might not be wrong about that.

But here's what I need you to hear, and I'm saying this to you not as a researcher or an author but as someone in the community who has watched this play out time and time again: the type of DL behavior does not determine the severity of the betrayal. A woman whose husband had one anonymous encounter with a man on Grindr has been betrayed. A woman whose husband maintained a four-year emotional relationship with a trans woman has been betrayed. The pain is real in both cases. The violation of trust is real in both cases. And in both cases, you deserve honesty, accountability, and the space to make your own decisions about what happens next.

What is different, and what matters for your decision-making, is the nature of what you're dealing with. The woman in the first scenario is dealing with a man who has a sexual behavior he's hiding. The woman in the second scenario is potentially dealing with a man who has a whole emotional and romantic life he's hiding. These require different conversations with different therapists using different frameworks. And that's not just my opinion, it's the practical reality that women in both situations have shared with me.

I also want to address something that often gets lost in these conversations: neither type of DL man set out to hurt you. I know that might be hard to hear right now. I know anger is easier than empathy. And I'm not asking you to forgive, that's your choice, and it's a choice that belongs entirely to you, on your timeline. But I am asking you to understand that the man you're dealing with is also a product of a culture that told him his desires were unacceptable, a church that told him his attraction was sinful, a community that told him he'd lose everything if the truth came out. He chose secrecy because, in his world, secrecy felt like the only option. That doesn't make it right. But it does make it human.

And understanding the humanity in it, on all sides, yours included, is what's going to get you through this. Not rage alone. Not shame alone. Not confusion alone. Understanding. That's what this book is building, chapter by chapter. And if you're still here, reading, processing, sitting with these stories and these facts, then you're already doing the work.

Neither situation is better or worse than the other. Both involve deception, and both put you at risk, emotionally and potentially physically. But they require different conversations, different approaches, and different frameworks for decision-making. And that's why this book exists: to give you the specific framework that matches your specific reality, rather than a one-size-fits-all approach that was designed for a different situation.

In the next chapter, we're going to go even deeper into what makes the second type tick, specifically, the role that feminine presentation plays as the key trigger of attraction. We'll talk about the hair, the nails, the body, and the investment that goes into creating the kind of femininity that draws these men in. Because understanding what he's attracted to is the next step in understanding why this happened, and ultimately, in deciding what you're going to do about it.

Before you move on, though, sit with Monique's words for a minute. She told me something at the end of our conversation that I think every woman reading this book needs to hear:

"The hardest part was that the world gave me a script for my first DL experience and no script at all for my second one. If this book had existed when I was going through it with Derek, I would have understood what I was dealing with so much sooner. And understanding it sooner means you start healing sooner. That's all I want for the next woman: to understand it sooner."

That's what we're building here, one chapter at a time. Keep reading.

CHAPTER FOUR

The Hair, the Nails, the Body: Why Feminine Presentation Is the Key

Let me paint you a picture. A trans woman walks into a restaurant in Buckhead. Her lace front is laid, thirty inches of body wave, parted to perfection, not a track showing. Her makeup is editorial: soft matte foundation, contoured cheekbones, a brown nude lip, lashes that flutter when she blinks. Her nails are coffin-shaped acrylics, nude with a French tip, freshly filled. Her skin is smooth as a magazine cover, arms, legs, chest, face, not a shadow of stubble anywhere. She's wearing a fitted midi dress that follows every curve, heels that add four inches to her frame, and a handbag that matches. She smells expensive. She moves like she knows people are watching, and she doesn't care.

Every man in that restaurant looked. Every single one. Not because they clocked her as trans. Most of them didn't. They looked because she was a strikingly beautiful, meticulously put-together woman, and men look at strikingly beautiful women. It's not complicated. It's not political. It's the oldest story in human history: femininity, when it's done at a high level, commands attention.

Now, I'm describing this to you in detail for a reason. This chapter is about the feminine presentation itself, the hair, the nails, the skin, the body, the clothes, the walk, the energy, and why it is the single most important factor in the attraction pattern we've been discussing throughout this book. Not biology. Not chromosomes. Not what's under the dress. The presentation. The femininity as it is seen, experienced, and responded to. Because for the DL men this book is about, the presentation is everything.

The Investment: What It Takes to Build This Level of Femininity

Before we talk about why feminine presentation triggers attraction, you need to understand what it takes to create it. Because this is not a casual effort. The level of femininity that attracts DL men: the level that makes them risk their marriages, their reputations, and their standing in the community, represents an investment of time, money, skill, and dedication that most cisgender women would find staggering.

Let me break it down, because the details matter.

The Hair

Hair is the crown. Ask any trans woman or femboy what the single most important element of their feminine presentation is, and most will say the hair before anything else. And they're not talking about a wig from the beauty supply store around the corner. The women and femboys who attract serious DL male attention are investing in high-quality human hair lace front wigs, custom units, or sew-in weaves that cost anywhere from three hundred to over a thousand dollars per unit. Many own multiple units for different looks and occasions. The wigs are customized: bleached knots, plucked hairlines, tinted lace that matches their skin tone, baby hairs laid with precision. Some invest in frontal wigs with invisible grid lace that creates the illusion of a natural hairline so convincing you could stare at it from six inches away and not know it's a wig.

The maintenance is ongoing. A quality wig needs to be washed, conditioned, and restyled regularly. A sew-in needs touch-ups every four to six weeks. For trans women who grow their own hair, the investment shifts to salon visits, treatments, and styling products. Either way, the annual cost for hair alone can run into the thousands; and for the women who maintain multiple units in rotation, easily five figures a year.

Why does this matter for the attraction conversation? Because hair is the single most powerful visual signifier of femininity in our culture. Long, styled, flowing hair reads as feminine immediately, unconsciously, and powerfully. It frames the face, softens the features, and creates a silhouette that the brain associates with womanhood before any other feature registers. When DL men describe what attracts them, hair is almost always the first thing mentioned. Not sometimes. Almost always.

The Skin

After hair, the next investment is skin. And by skin, I mean the removal of everything that signals masculinity: body hair, facial hair, and the shadow that stubble leaves even when freshly shaved. For trans women on hormone therapy, estrogen gradually reduces body hair growth over time, but it rarely eliminates it completely. Most trans women supplement hormones with laser hair removal, electrolysis, or regular waxing. Laser hair removal for the face alone can require six to twelve sessions at a hundred to three hundred dollars per session. Full-body treatments multiply that cost significantly. Electrolysis, which provides permanent removal one hair at a time, can cost over ten thousand dollars and require dozens of hours over multiple years.

Femboys who have not undergone hormone therapy face an even more labor-intensive process, managing body hair through daily or near-daily shaving, regular waxing appointments, or a combination of both. The goal is the same: smooth, soft skin that reads as feminine to the eye and to the touch.

And then there's skincare. Not just washing your face with whatever's in the shower. I'm talking about multi-step routines: cleansers, serums, moisturizers, sunscreen, retinol, chemical exfoliants. Trans women and dedicated femboys often maintain skincare regimens that rival those of professional beauty influencers, because soft, clear, glowing skin is another powerful marker of femininity. The texture of the skin, the way it catches light, the absence of roughness, all of it contributes to the overall feminine impression that triggers attraction.

The Nails

Nails might seem like a small detail, but in this world, they're not small at all. They're a signal. Long, manicured nails, acrylics, gel extensions, press-ons done well, instantly communicate femininity. They change the way a person gestures, holds their phone, picks up a glass. They catch the light. They make a sound when they tap a surface. Nails are one of the first things DL men notice and one of the features they consistently mention when describing what draws them in.

The cost of maintaining quality nails isn't trivial either. A full set of custom acrylics can run forty to a hundred dollars or more, with fills needed every two to three weeks. Designs, charms, and custom nail art add to the cost. Over the course of a year, a woman who keeps her nails consistently done is spending anywhere from a thousand to three thousand dollars, on her fingertips alone.

The Makeup

If hair is the crown, makeup is the magic. And I say that as someone who has watched queens and trans women transform themselves in real time, I've been backstage at pageants, in dressing rooms before balls, in apartments where a friend sat at her vanity and went from masculine to breathtaking in ninety minutes. Makeup, applied with skill, is the single most powerful tool for creating the visual illusion of femininity. It can reshape the face, soften the jaw, lift the cheekbones, enlarge the eyes, feminize the brow, and create a symmetry and softness that reads as unmistakably female.

The women and femboys who attract DL men are not doing drugstore-counter makeup. They're executing professional-grade artistry. Full-coverage foundation matched precisely to skin tone. Color correction for beard shadow: a critical step for trans women who need to neutralize the blue-gray undertone that facial hair leaves even after a close shave. Contour and highlight to sculpt the nose, jawline, and cheekbones. Brows shaped and filled to frame the eyes. Professional-quality false lashes, or, increasingly, lash extensions maintained at a salon every two to three weeks at sixty to a hundred dollars per fill. Lip liner and color applied to create the illusion of fuller, softer lips.

Many of these individuals have spent years watching tutorials, practicing techniques, and investing in professional-grade products.

A quality makeup collection for this level of application can easily run into the hundreds or thousands of dollars. And the time investment is significant: a full beat for a night out can take sixty to ninety minutes or more. Some trans women maintain a lighter "everyday" face for daytime and bring out the full artistry for dates, events, and social outings, creating two distinct levels of feminine presentation depending on the context.

The Walk, the Voice, the Energy

And then there are the intangibles: the elements of feminine presentation that can't be bought or surgically created. The way a person walks: the hip sway, the shorter stride, the heel-toe placement that comes naturally in heels. The way a person sits: legs crossed, hands in the lap, posture that communicates softness rather than dominance. The voice: some trans women undergo vocal training to raise their pitch, soften their resonance, and adopt speech patterns that read as feminine. Others have naturally higher voices that require minimal adjustment. And then there's the energy: the way a person makes you feel when you're in their presence. Feminine energy is gentle, warm, receptive, sometimes playful, sometimes coy. It's the laugh, the way she touches your arm when she talks, the way she looks at you through her lashes.

DL men talk about this energy as much as they talk about the physical presentation. One man told me: "It's not just how she looks. It's how she makes me feel. When I'm with her, I feel like a man.

She makes me feel masculine because she's so feminine. That dynamic, that polarity, is what I'm addicted to." That polarity he's describing is the essence of what drives this attraction. These men are responding to the full experience of femininity: visual, physical, emotional, energetic. And the trans women and femboys who have mastered all of these dimensions create an experience that is, for these men, profoundly compelling.

The Body

This is where the investment becomes most significant; and most personal. For trans women, achieving a feminine body shape often involves a combination of hormone therapy, diet and exercise, and in many cases, surgical procedures. Hormone replacement therapy, which typically involves estrogen and an anti-androgen medication, costs anywhere from forty to four hundred dollars per month and produces gradual changes: breast development, fat redistribution to the hips and thighs, softening of facial features, and a reduction in muscle mass. These changes take months to years to fully manifest.

For many trans women, hormones alone don't achieve the body shape they desire, and they pursue surgical options. Breast augmentation can cost five thousand to ten thousand dollars. Facial feminization surgery: a set of procedures that may include brow bone reduction, rhinoplasty, jaw contouring, and lip augmentation, can run twenty thousand to fifty thousand dollars or more. Body contouring procedures like liposuction or Brazilian butt lifts add additional costs. When you total up the potential investment in surgical feminization, the number for a comprehensive transformation can exceed a hundred thousand dollars over the course of several years.

Femboys, who generally don't pursue surgical modification, achieve a feminine body aesthetic through different means: waist trainers, hip padding, strategic clothing choices, targeted exercise routines, and in some cases, hormones taken outside of medical supervision: a risky but not uncommon practice. The goal is the same: to create a visual impression of feminine curves, a soft body, and a silhouette that reads as female.

Nova's Story

Nova is a twenty-six-year-old trans woman in Los Angeles who makes a living as a beauty influencer with over two hundred thousand followers across platforms. She transitioned at nineteen and has spent, by her own estimate, over ninety thousand dollars on her appearance over seven years. That includes hormones, facial feminization surgery, breast augmentation, laser hair removal, a professional wig collection, and a beauty routine that takes two hours every morning.

"People see me and they see a beautiful woman," Nova told me. "They don't see the investment. They don't see the hours, the pain, the money. They just see the result. And the men who pursue me? They especially don't see it. They just see a woman they want. And honestly, that's the point. I didn't go through all of this so people could clock me. I went through it so people could see me as I am."

Nova has dated multiple DL men. She's matter-of-fact about it. "They love the presentation. They love the hair, the face, the body, the way I carry myself. One of my exes, married man, two kids, used to tell me I was more feminine than his wife. Not to be cruel. He meant it as a compliment. He genuinely saw me as the most feminine person in his life, and that femininity is what made him unable to stay away."

I asked Nova what she thought cisgender women needed to understand about the investment trans women make in their appearance. She laughed. "That we work harder at it than most people can imagine. I'm not saying that to brag. I'm saying it because when a woman finds out her man is seeing a trans girl who looks like she belongs on a magazine cover, that woman needs to understand: that magazine-cover look didn't happen by accident. It's a full-time job. And the result of that job is a level of femininity that is, in some ways, heightened beyond what most cisgender women maintain; because for us, it's not just about looking good. It's about being seen as who we are."

Heightened Femininity: When More Is More

Here's where this chapter makes a turn that might be uncomfortable, but it's necessary. One of the patterns that emerged consistently in the Northwestern University research, in the conversations I've had with DL men, and in the observations of trans women and femboys themselves is this: many DL men are not just attracted to femininity. They are attracted to heightened femininity, femininity that is curated, amplified, and polished to a degree that exceeds what they typically encounter in their day-to-day lives.

I want to be careful here because I'm not saying cisgender women aren't feminine. Of course they are. I'm not saying cisgender women don't invest in their appearance. Many do, beautifully. What I'm saying is that for the trans women and femboys who attract DL male attention, the feminine presentation is often intentionally dialed up to a level that goes beyond the everyday. The wigs are longer and more styled than most women's natural hair. The nails are longer and more elaborate. The makeup is more precisely applied. The clothing is more fitted, more form-hugging, more deliberately sexy. The entire aesthetic is turned up to eleven, not because these individuals are performing a caricature of womanhood, but because, for many of them, achieving femininity required so much effort that the result is a concentrated, almost distilled version of feminine presentation.

Researchers who study sexual attraction have long understood that exaggerated sexual characteristics tend to produce stronger arousal responses. This is known in evolutionary psychology as the superstimulus effect: the idea that an artificial stimulus that amplifies the features that trigger a natural response can produce an even stronger response than the natural stimulus itself. Think of it this way: if a man is attracted to curves, the person with the most pronounced curves will draw the most attention. If he's attracted to long hair, the longest, most luxurious hair will trigger the strongest response. If he's attracted to feminine energy, the most overtly feminine person in the room will pull his focus.

This is not a moral judgment. This is not about better or worse, real or fake, natural or artificial. This is about understanding the mechanics of attraction in the specific context we're discussing. The trans women and femboys who attract DL men are often producing what amounts to a superstimulus of femininity: a presentation so intensely feminine that it triggers a stronger-than-average attraction response in men who are wired to respond to feminine cues. And that heightened response is part of what makes the attraction feel, to the man experiencing it, so overwhelming and so difficult to resist.

Terrance's Story

Terrance is thirty-eight, lives in Chicago, and has been in a committed relationship with his girlfriend, Yvette, for six years. He came to me because he wanted someone in the community who might understand what he was going through without judging him. His secret: a two-year on-and-off involvement with a trans woman named Paris who he met through Instagram.

"I need you to understand what happened the first time I saw her," Terrance said. "I was scrolling through my Explore page and her picture came up. Just a selfie. Hair done, face done, outfit on point. And my body reacted. Not my mind, my body. Before I even read the caption, before I knew anything about her, my body had already decided. She was the most feminine thing I had ever seen in my life. More than Yvette. More than any woman I'd ever dated. And I know that sounds terrible, but it's the truth."

Terrance slid into Paris's DMs. They talked for weeks before meeting. When they finally met in person, Terrance said the attraction was even more intense. "In person, she was flawless. Her skin was like butter. Her nails were perfect. Her hair moved when she walked. She smelled like a garden. And the way she carried herself, soft, graceful, feminine in every gesture, I was done. I was absolutely done."

When I asked Terrance to articulate specifically what made Paris's femininity so powerful compared to the femininity of cisgender women he'd been with, he struggled for a moment, then said something that I think captures the heart of this chapter: "It's like the difference between someone who sings naturally and someone who has trained their voice for years. Yvette is naturally feminine, she's beautiful, she doesn't have to try. Paris's femininity is crafted. Every single thing about her appearance has been thought about, worked on, perfected. And that level of intentional femininity hits different. It just does."

Social Media and the Elevation of Feminine Presentation

We cannot have this conversation without talking about the role social media has played in elevating the visibility and the standard of feminine presentation among trans women and femboys. Because the internet didn't just make these individuals more accessible to DL men: it transformed the entire culture of feminine presentation in ways that directly feed into the attraction dynamic we're discussing.

Instagram, TikTok, YouTube, and Twitter have created an ecosystem where trans women and femboys can document, share, and monetize their femininity. Transition timelines, makeup tutorials, wig reviews, outfit-of-the-day posts, and "get ready with me" videos have turned the process of achieving femininity into content. And that content does two things simultaneously: it raises the standard of what's possible, and it puts the results directly in front of the eyes of men who are susceptible to the attraction.

Think about it from the DL man's perspective. Before social media, his exposure to highly feminine trans women or femboys was limited to whatever he might encounter in person, which, depending on where he lived, could be very little. Now, he has unlimited access to an endless feed of stunningly beautiful feminine-presenting individuals, curated and filtered for maximum visual impact, available twenty-four hours a day on the device in his pocket. The Instagram Explore page alone has introduced countless men to an attraction they didn't even know they had. The algorithm sees what you linger on, what you double-tap, what you save; and it gives you more of it. For a man with even a latent attraction to heightened femininity, the algorithm becomes a pipeline.

I've heard this story so many times it could be a template: "I wasn't looking for it. The algorithm just started showing me these beautiful women. And then I found out some of them were trans. And I couldn't stop looking." The algorithm didn't create the attraction. But it surfaced it, amplified it, and made it impossible to ignore.

And it's not just passive consumption. Social media has created a direct pipeline from admiration to pursuit. A man sees a beautiful trans woman on his Explore page. He follows her. He likes a few photos. He saves a post. Then one night, emboldened by loneliness or desire or the false courage that comes from a screen, he sends a DM. And that DM is the beginning of the secret life. I have talked to trans women who receive dozens of DMs a week from married men, men who found them through nothing more than the Instagram algorithm doing it's job. The technology has made the pipeline from latent attraction to active pursuit shorter and smoother than it has ever been in human history.

For women, this means something important: your man's involvement with trans women or femboys may not have started with a deliberate search. He may not have gone looking for this. The algorithm may have brought it to him, and his own psychology took it from there. That doesn't excuse the choices he made afterward: he chose to follow, to DM, to pursue, to lie. But it does help explain how a man with no previous awareness of this attraction can find himself, seemingly out of nowhere, deep in a secret relationship with someone his wife never imagined he'd be attracted to.

Whitney's Story

Whitney is a thirty-one-year-old femboy in New Orleans with a significant social media following. Whitney doesn't identify as a woman, uses they/them pronouns, but presents in a hyper-feminine aesthetic that attracts enormous attention from men, including a steady stream of DL men in committed relationships with women.

"My DMs are a whole other world," Whitney told me, laughing. "Married men, engaged men, men with their family photos right there in their profile, sliding into my DMs at two in the morning telling me I'm the most beautiful person they've ever seen. And they're not just complimenting. They're pursuing. Hard. They want to meet. They want to date. They want to fly me out. One man offered to put me in an apartment."

Whitney showed me a selection of the messages, with identifying details blacked out, and they were striking in their consistency. The men focused almost exclusively on Whitney's appearance: the hair, the nails, the skin, the body, the outfits. Multiple men used the word "feminine" explicitly. Several said variations of "You're more feminine than my girl." One wrote: "I don't even know how to explain what you do to me. I've never been attracted to a man before but you're not a man to me. You're the most feminine person I've ever seen."

"That last message is the most common thing I hear," Whitney said. "They don't see me as a man. They don't see masculinity when they look at me. They see femininity, pure, concentrated femininity, and that's what they're responding to. The fact that I was assigned male at birth is irrelevant to their attraction. Their eyes, their bodies, their desire, all of it is responding to the femininity, not to the biology underneath it."

The Passing Spectrum: Where Attraction and Presentation Intersect

I need to talk about "passing" for a moment, and I want to do it honestly while acknowledging that the concept is contentious within the LGBTQIA community. Passing refers to how convincingly a trans person presents as their identified gender, essentially, whether a stranger on the street would perceive them as cisgender. Some trans activists argue that the concept of passing reinforces cisnormative beauty standards and suggests that trans women are only valid when they look "like real women." I hear that critique, and it's valid.

But in the context of this book, we have to discuss passing honestly because it directly relates to the attraction dynamic we're examining. The research from Northwestern University found a clear pattern: the more feminine the presentation, the stronger the attraction response from the men being studied. This isn't about ranking trans women on a scale of worthiness. It's about understanding the mechanics of attraction in the specific population of men this book addresses.

DL men who pursue trans women and femboys are overwhelmingly attracted to individuals who pass convincingly as cisgender women, or, in the case of femboys, who present a level of femininity that makes their assigned sex difficult to detect at a glance. This is consistent with the central thesis of this book: these men are attracted to femininity, and the more fully realized the femininity, the more powerful the attraction.

This creates a hierarchy within the DL dating world that mirrors, in uncomfortable ways, the beauty hierarchies that exist everywhere else. The trans women who attract the most DL male attention tend to be the ones who have invested the most heavily in their presentation: the surgical enhancements, the premium wigs, the professional-grade makeup skills, the hormone regimens that have reshaped their bodies over years. The femboys who attract the most attention tend to be the ones who can achieve a "soft" or "androgynous-to-feminine" look that makes people do a double take. And the drag queens who attract genuine romantic or sexual interest, as opposed to artistic appreciation, tend to be the ones whose transformations are the most seamless and convincing.

For the woman reading this, the passing dynamic means something specific and painful: the person your man is attracted to probably doesn't look like what you expected. You may have been expecting to find evidence of your man talking to someone who is obviously trans, obviously male underneath, obviously "different." Instead, you're probably looking at photos of someone who looks like any other beautiful woman on Instagram. And that disconnect, between what you expected and what you found, is part of what makes this discovery so disorienting.

Carmen's Story

Carmen is a forty-year-old trans woman in Miami who has been fully transitioned for twelve years. She had facial feminization surgery at twenty-nine, breast augmentation at thirty-one, and maintains what she describes as "a non-negotiable commitment to my presentation." Carmen is, by any measure, a strikingly beautiful woman. She works as a real estate agent, and most of her clients and colleagues have no idea she is trans.

"I've dated DL men for most of my adult life," Carmen told me. "Not by choice, really, it's just the reality. The men who are attracted to me are almost always in relationships with women, almost always DL, and almost always drawn to me because of what they see on the outside. I've had men tell me, point blank, that they wouldn't be attracted to a trans woman who didn't look the way I look. They're not attracted to 'trans.' They're attracted to beautiful women. And I happen to be a beautiful woman who is also trans."

Carmen is clear-eyed about how this dynamic plays out. "The men who come to me have a type, and that type is: looks like a cisgender woman. If I walked around with no wig, no makeup, no effort? They wouldn't look twice. It's the presentation. It's always the presentation. And I don't say that to diminish myself, I am who I am regardless of how I look. But in terms of what attracts these specific men? It's the visual. It's the femininity they can see. Full stop."

I asked Carmen what she would say to a cisgender woman who was struggling with feeling "out-feminined" by a trans woman. Her answer was compassionate: "I would say that the femininity she has is hers by birthright and nobody can take that from her. What I have is something I built, brick by brick, over years. Both are valid. Both are real. And the fact that her man is attracted to both of us tells you something about him, not about either of us. We're not each other's enemies. We're both dealing with a man who lied."

The Uncomfortable Truth for Cisgender Women

I promised at the beginning of this book that I would tell you the truth, even the parts that hurt. So here it is: some of these men find the heightened femininity of trans women and femboys more visually compelling than the natural femininity of the cisgender women in their lives. That is not a judgment of you. That is not a reflection of your worth, your beauty, or your femininity. But it is a reality that you need to understand if you're going to make sense of what you're dealing with.

The woman at home is naturally feminine. She doesn't have to fight for it, doesn't have to construct it from the ground up, doesn't have to invest tens of thousands of dollars to achieve it. Her femininity is effortless because it's innate. And for most purposes, that effortless femininity is exactly what attracts men. But the DL men we're discussing have discovered a version of femininity that is not effortless: a version that is deliberate, curated, and polished to an extraordinary degree. And the deliberateness of it, the sheer effort and artistry behind it, produces a result that is, in some ways, a more intense expression of the very thing these men are wired to respond to.

Now, I know some women reading this are feeling some type of way right now. You might be feeling angry, inadequate, confused, or all three at once. I get it. And I want you to hear me say this clearly: you are not in competition with these trans women and femboys.

You are not losing to them. This is not a contest. The fact that your man responds to a heightened form of femininity does not mean your femininity is insufficient. It means his wiring is broader than you were told to expect. It means his attraction spans a wider range of feminine expression than the culture prepared you for. That's his reality to deal with. Not yours.

What is yours to deal with is the decision about what to do with this information. And that decision requires clarity: the kind of clarity that only comes from understanding exactly what you're facing. Which is what these chapters are giving you.

The Craft of Femininity: Why Intentional Beauty Resonates

There's a psychological dimension to this that goes beyond simple visual stimulation, and I think it's worth exploring because it helps explain why these men aren't just physically attracted, they're often emotionally captivated.

When a trans woman or a femboy invests heavily in their feminine presentation, the result isn't just a beautiful appearance. It's an expression of identity, desire, and intention. Every element of the presentation was chosen. The specific shade of the lip color. The length and shape of the nails. The style of the wig. The cut of the dress. Nothing is accidental. Everything is deliberate. And that deliberateness communicates something powerful: this person cares deeply about femininity. They've devoted themselves to it. They've sacrificed for it. They've made it the center of their self-expression.

For some DL men, that devotion to femininity is itself attractive. It signals something beyond beauty: it signals an intensity of feminine commitment that they find irresistible. One man I spoke with put it this way: "My wife is beautiful, but she doesn't think about her femininity. It's just there. The trans women I've been with live femininity. They breathe it. Every choice they make is a choice to be more feminine. And that energy, that intentional femininity, is what draws me in."

I want to be careful not to romanticize this, because at the end of the day, this man is still lying to his wife. But understanding what he's experiencing helps explain why the attraction feels, to him, so different from a typical affair. He's not just attracted to a person. He's attracted to an ideal of femininity that has been made real through extraordinary effort. And that's a powerful thing to be drawn to.

As we move into the next chapter, which focuses on how these DL men actually operate their secret lives, the day-to-day mechanics of maintaining the deception, keep this chapter's core message in mind: the key to this attraction is femininity itself. Not biology. Not anatomy. Femininity as it is seen, felt, and experienced. The hair, the nails, the skin, the body, the walk, the energy. These are the elements that light the fire. And once that fire is lit, as the next chapter will show you, these men build entire architectures of secrecy to keep it burning.

Understanding the fuel helps you understand the fire. And understanding the fire helps you decide how to protect yourself from getting burned.

A Final Word: Lorraine's Realization

Lorraine is fifty-three and lives in Birmingham, Alabama. When she discovered that her husband, Bernard, had been involved with a trans woman for nearly five years, her first reaction was to search for photos of the other woman. What she found changed the way she understood her entire situation.

"She was gorgeous," Lorraine told me, her voice quiet but steady. "That was the first thing I had to deal with, before I dealt with the betrayal, before I dealt with the anger, before I dealt with anything else, I had to sit with the fact that this woman was drop-dead gorgeous. Her hair was down to her waist. Her skin was perfect. Her nails were always done. Her outfits were… impeccable. I stared at those photos for hours. Not because I was comparing myself to her. Because I was trying to understand what my husband saw. And what I finally understood was: he saw a woman. A beautiful, feminine, put-together woman. He didn't see a man in a dress. He saw what I would see if I passed her in the mall: a woman who had her stuff together."

Lorraine paused, then said something that stopped me cold: "The thing nobody prepared me for was that I couldn't hate her. I wanted to. Believe me, I wanted to. But how do you hate someone for being beautiful? How do you hate someone for investing in themselves? How do you hate someone who, from everything I could see, was just living her life and happened to attract my husband? The person I had to deal with was him. Not her. She didn't owe me anything. He owed me everything."

That clarity: the ability to separate the anger at the betrayal from the reality of the attraction, is exactly what this chapter is trying to give you. The hair, the nails, the body, the skin, the walk, the energy, these are the elements that drew your man in. Understanding them doesn't make the betrayal hurt less. But it does help you aim your pain in the right direction: at the man who lied, not at the person he lied with, and not at yourself.

In the next chapter, we're going to pull back the curtain on the day-to-day mechanics of how DL men who pursue feminine-presenting individuals actually operate: the apps, the routines, the lies, the financial trails, and the emotional gymnastics they perform to maintain their double lives. If this chapter was about understanding the "why," the next chapter is about understanding the "how." And the "how" is where the practical tools for protecting yourself begin.

But take a breath before you turn that page. You've just absorbed a lot, about the investment, the beauty, the heightened femininity, the algorithm, and the uncomfortable reality that your man may have found himself drawn to a version of femininity that is more deliberately crafted than anything he encounters in his everyday life. None of that is your fault. None of that is your failing. And the fact that you're here, reading, learning, and refusing to accept confusion as a permanent state: that tells me everything I need to know about the kind of woman you are. You're the kind who fights for clarity. So let's keep fighting.

CHAPTER FIVE

His Secret Life: How DL Men Who Pursue Feminine-Presenting Individuals Operate

If the last four chapters gave you the "why," this chapter gives you the "how." And I'm going to be specific. Not vague, not theoretical, not wrapped in euphemisms. Specific. Because you didn't pick up this book to hear generalities, you picked it up because you need to know exactly how the man in your life has been operating behind your back, so you can make informed decisions about what to do next.

This chapter is a blueprint of the secret life. I'm going to walk you through the digital infrastructure: the apps, the platforms, the accounts. I'm going to show you the financial architecture, how money moves and where it goes. I'm going to break down the time management, how he creates windows of opportunity without raising suspicion. I'm going to explain the emotional compartmentalization, how he keeps two realities running simultaneously without losing his mind. And I'm going to tell you about the role that travel and geography play in maintaining the illusion.

Everything in this chapter comes from the same place everything else in this book comes from: conversations with real people on all sides of this dynamic, DL men, the trans women and femboys they're involved with, and the women who eventually discovered the truth. I'm also drawing on my own observations as a member of the LGBTQIA community who has watched these dynamics play out in real time, in real spaces, in real lives.

Let's get into it.

The Digital Infrastructure: Apps, Accounts, and Aliases

The secret life begins online. Almost without exception, the DL men who pursue trans women and femboys in 2026 are operating within a digital ecosystem that their wives and girlfriends have no idea exists. And the sophistication of that digital infrastructure has evolved dramatically in recent years.

The Apps

Unlike DL men who pursue masculine men, who typically use apps like Grindr, Jack'd, or SCRUFF, the DL men in this category use a different set of platforms entirely. The most common include

Taimi, which bills itself as the world's largest LGBTQ+ dating and social networking app with over twenty-seven million users; Butterfly, a dating app built specifically for transgender people and those interested in dating them, which emphasizes privacy features like approximate locations and auto-deleting messages; Translr, designed specifically for trans dating; and My Transgender Cupid, which markets itself to men seeking serious relationships with trans women.

But here's what women need to understand: many of these men aren't exclusively using trans-specific apps. They're also using mainstream platforms, Tinder, Hinge, Bumble, and especially OkCupid, which offers over sixty gender identity options and allows users to filter their preferences in ways that can surface trans women in search results. A DL man on Tinder can adjust his preferences to include trans women without ever downloading a trans-specific app. And because Tinder is on everybody's phone; or at least, finding Tinder on your man's phone wouldn't necessarily raise the specific alarm that finding a trans dating app would: this strategy provides an additional layer of cover.

And then there's social media: the gateway drug. As we discussed in the previous chapter, Instagram, TikTok, and Twitter are where many DL men first encounter the trans women and femboys they eventually pursue. But social media isn't just a discovery platform. It's an active communication channel. DMs on

Instagram and Twitter are end-to-end encrypted. They leave no trace on phone bills. They can be accessed through private browsing. And for the DL man who wants to pursue someone he found on social media without downloading a dating app at all, sliding into the DMs is the most frictionless path from desire to connection.

The Burner Infrastructure

The men who have been doing this for more than a few months almost always develop a burner infrastructure. This can include a second phone: a prepaid device purchased with cash, with its own number and its own set of apps, that lives in the car, in a gym bag, at the office, or in some other location the wife never checks. It can include secondary email addresses created specifically for dating app registrations: a Gmail or ProtonMail account tied to a fake name. It can include secondary social media accounts: a private Instagram with no profile picture, following nothing but trans women and femboy influencers; a Twitter account with a pseudonym, used to interact with trans content creators. And it often includes communication apps that offer enhanced privacy, Telegram, Signal, WhatsApp with disappearing messages enabled, chosen specifically because they are harder to surveil than standard text messaging.

I've sat with trans women who showed me their message threads with DL men, and the operational security these men employ would impress a spy novelist. Specific instructions about when to text and when not to. Code names stored in the phone as plausible contacts, "Johnny from the gym," "Mike at work." Conversations set to auto-delete after twenty-four hours. Calls made only during specific windows: the commute to work, the lunch break, late at night after the wife has gone to sleep. The level of planning and discipline is remarkable, and it tells you something important about the intensity of the attraction: a man doesn't build this kind of infrastructure for a casual curiosity. He builds it because the pull is strong enough to justify the effort and the risk.

Darnell's Story

Darnell is forty-three and works as a regional sales manager in the Midwest. He's been married for sixteen years. His wife, Angela, is a stay-at-home mother of their three children. Darnell agreed to talk to me because he says he's tired of carrying the weight alone.

Darnell's burner infrastructure is a masterpiece of deception. He has a second phone: a Samsung he bought at Walmart for sixty dollars, with a prepaid SIM card. It lives in his car, tucked into a compartment under the center console that Angela has never noticed. The phone has Taimi, a private Instagram account, and Telegram installed. The Instagram account follows eighty-seven trans women and femboy influencers. The Telegram has active conversations with three trans women he's been involved with over the past four years.

"I know it sounds crazy," Darnell told me. "A whole second phone. But you have to understand, if Angela ever found this on my regular phone, my life would be over. My marriage, my church, my standing in the community, my relationship with my kids, all of it. So yeah, I have a second phone. And I check it every single day."

Darnell's primary relationship is with a trans woman named Imani who lives two hours away. They see each other twice a month, always on days when Darnell has "client meetings" in her city. He books the hotel on a personal credit card that Angela doesn't have access to. He pays for dinners in cash. He keeps a change of clothes at Imani's apartment. The relationship has been going on for two and a half years, and Darnell describes it as "the most honest relationship I've ever had, ironic as that sounds, given that the whole thing is built on lies."

Follow the Money: The Financial Architecture of the Secret Life

Money talks, and in the world of DL relationships with trans women and femboys, it talks loud. One of the most reliable indicators that something is going on is unexplained financial activity; and the DL men in this category tend to leave a bigger financial footprint than those involved in anonymous hookups, precisely because they're maintaining ongoing relationships that require ongoing investment.

The financial flows take several forms. Direct transfers through cash apps are the most common. Venmo, CashApp, Zelle, and PayPal are the vehicles of choice, and the payments often follow a predictable pattern: regular transfers of consistent amounts, a hundred dollars every Friday, two hundred on the first of the month, that function like an allowance or stipend. These payments are sometimes framed as "helping out" a friend, and the man may have a cover story ready for each one. But the regularity and consistency of the payments tell a different story than occasional friendly generosity.

Beyond direct transfers, there are the expenses associated with maintaining the relationship itself. Hotel rooms for their rendezvous, booked on secondary credit cards or paid in cash. Restaurant bills. Gift purchases: wigs, clothing, jewelry, electronics. Some men pay their partner's rent, either partially or in full. Some pay for beauty expenses, nail appointments, hair installations, skincare products. I spoke with one trans woman who told me her DL boyfriend spent over thirty thousand dollars on her in a single year, and he did it by skimming from his family's finances in amounts small enough that his wife didn't notice any single transaction but large enough that the total was staggering.

For the woman trying to understand where the money is going, here's what to look for: unexplained cash withdrawals, especially in round numbers and regular intervals. Cash app transactions to names or usernames you don't recognize. A secondary credit card you didn't know about; or charges on a known card that don't match his stated whereabouts. Gift purchases he can't explain. And the absence of spending where there should be some, for instance, if he claims he went to dinner with clients but there's no restaurant charge on the card, because he paid cash to avoid the paper trail.

Nicole's Story

Nicole is a forty-one-year-old accountant in Jacksonville. Her professional eye for numbers is exactly what led her to discover her husband Raymond's secret life. "I noticed it the way I'd notice a discrepancy in a client's books," she told me. "It just didn't add up."

The first red flag was ATM withdrawals. Raymond had started pulling two hundred dollars in cash every week, consistently, like clockwork. When Nicole asked about it, he said he was tipping a trainer at the gym. Then she noticed that their grocery budget kept coming in under what she'd allocated, because Raymond was eating "late dinners at work" several nights a week, dinners that didn't show up on any credit card statement.

Nicole started digging. She found a CashApp account linked to an email address she'd never seen. The account showed regular payments to someone with the username "QueenBee." Over the course of eighteen months, the payments totaled just over eleven thousand dollars. "Eleven thousand dollars," Nicole repeated, her voice flat. "While I was over here counting coupons for school supplies."

The person behind "QueenBee" was a trans woman named Bianca who lived forty-five minutes away. Raymond had been seeing her for almost two years. He had been paying a portion of her rent, covering her hair and nail appointments, and taking her shopping. "He was funding a whole lifestyle," Nicole said. "And he was doing it with our money. Money that was supposed to go to our kids, our mortgage, our future. He was investing in a relationship with someone else while telling me we couldn't afford a family vacation."

Nicole's experience is far from unique. I've heard variations of this story from women across the country, women who discovered that their family's finances had been quietly diverted to fund their man's secret relationship. The amounts vary, but the pattern is consistent: regular outflows, cleverly disguised, draining from the household over months and years. One woman told me her husband had opened a credit card in her name, without her knowledge, to finance gifts for a trans woman he was seeing. Another discovered that her husband's "work expenses" reimbursement checks were actually being deposited into a separate account he used exclusively for his secret life.

The financial betrayal compounds the emotional betrayal in ways that can feel particularly devastating. It's one thing to learn your man was seeing someone else. It's another thing entirely to learn he was using the family's resources to do it: that every dinner you skipped, every vacation you postponed, every bill you stressed over might have been unnecessary if the money hadn't been flowing somewhere else. The financial dimension turns the betrayal from personal to practical, affecting not just your heart but your family's material reality.

For the woman trying to understand where the money is going, here are the patterns that show up most consistently: unexplained cash withdrawals, especially in round numbers and regular intervals. Cash app transactions to names or usernames you don't recognize. A secondary credit card you didn't know about; or charges on a known card that don't match his stated whereabouts. Gift purchases he can't explain, if you find receipts for wigs, acrylic nail sets, women's clothing, or beauty products that never showed up in your house, that's a significant red flag. And watch for the absence of spending where there should be some: if he claims he went to dinner with clients but there's no restaurant charge on the card, he may have paid cash to avoid the paper trail.

The Clock Game: How He Creates Time for the Secret Life

Money is one half of the equation. Time is the other. And the DL man who is maintaining an ongoing relationship with a trans woman or femboy has to become an expert in creating time windows, blocks of hours that are accounted for in his public life but actually devoted to his secret one.

The most common cover stories follow predictable patterns. Work-related excuses are the gold standard: late meetings, out-of-town client visits, work dinners, Saturday morning calls that require him to "go into the office." For men who travel for work, business trips become the perfect cover. A two-day conference in another city provides a built-in alibi and a hotel room that's already being paid for by the company. I've heard from trans women who said their DL partners would extend business trips by a day, telling the wife the conference ran long while actually spending the extra twenty-four hours with them.

The gym is another favorite. A man who suddenly starts going to the gym five or six times a week, especially if the sessions seem to last ninety minutes to two hours, may be using the gym as a time block that his wife doesn't question. He goes to the gym, works out for thirty minutes, spends an hour with his partner, comes home sweaty and tired. The cover is built into the activity.

Running errands that take too long is another telltale pattern. A trip to Home Depot that takes three hours. A car wash that somehow requires an entire Saturday morning. A visit to a friend's house that stretches from afternoon into evening. None of these are inherently suspicious in isolation. But when they become a pattern, when there's a recurring, unexplained block of time every week or every other week: the pattern itself becomes the clue.

And then there's the nighttime. Late-night phone activity, texting in bed after the wife has fallen asleep, stepping outside for a "cigarette" or a "phone call from work" at eleven o'clock at night, disappearing into the bathroom for extended periods with his phone. These are the moments when the second life bleeds into the first, and they're often the moments that first trigger a woman's suspicion.

Angela and Travis's Story

Angela is thirty-five and lives in Indianapolis. Her husband Travis is a long-haul truck driver: a profession that, as Angela now understands, provided the perfect cover for a secret life that had been running for nearly five years.

"He was gone three to four days a week," Angela told me. "I never questioned it. That's his job. He drives routes across three states. But what I didn't know was that one of his regular stops wasn't a truck stop or a warehouse. It was an apartment in Louisville where a trans woman named Destiny lived. He had a key. He kept clothes there. He had photos of them together on his burner phone, selfies at restaurants, walking through a park, sitting on her couch watching TV. It was a whole second household."

Angela discovered the truth when Travis was hospitalized after a minor accident on the road. She went through his truck to collect his personal belongings and found the second phone in the glove compartment. "I opened it and my whole marriage fell apart in five minutes," she said. "Five years of photos. Five years of text messages. Five years of 'I love you, baby.' He had told this woman he loved her. He had told her he was going to leave me eventually. He had made promises to her about a future together. And every single week, he came home to me and the kids and acted like nothing was happening."

Travis's job didn't create his attraction. But it created the perfect conditions for acting on it, long stretches of time away from home, a built-in excuse for being unreachable, and a route that conveniently passed through the city where his partner lived. For women whose men travel regularly for work, Angela's story is a cautionary example of how professional obligations can become the scaffolding for a secret life.

The Double Mind: How He Keeps Two Realities Running

The question I hear most often from women who've discovered their man's secret life isn't about the apps, the money, or the time. It's this: "How could he come home and look me in the eye?" It's a fair question. And the answer lies in something psychologists call compartmentalization: the ability to separate your mental life into distinct, non-overlapping sections that don't interact with each other.

Compartmentalization is a defense mechanism. It allows a person to hold two contradictory realities simultaneously without the emotional breakdown that should logically result. The DL man who is maintaining a loving, committed relationship with his wife while simultaneously maintaining a loving, committed relationship with a trans woman is not unaware of the contradiction. He knows it's there. But his mind has built walls between the two realities that allow him to be fully present in each one without the other intruding.

When he's at home with you, cooking dinner, helping with homework, watching television on the couch, in that moment, you are his reality. His partner, his other life, doesn't exist. Not because he's forgotten about it, but because his mind has filed it in a separate compartment that isn't active right now. And when he's with her, sitting across the table at a restaurant, holding her hand in his car, texting her goodnight, you don't exist in that compartment either. He's not thinking about your face. He's not wracked with guilt in that moment. He's present with her, fully, because the wall between the two compartments is holding.

This is why the discovery feels so shocking. Not just because he was lying, but because he seemed so normal. So present. So genuinely there. Because he was there. The compartmentalization was working. And the better it works, the more convincing the performance, which means the more devastating the reveal.

But compartmentalization has limits. Over time, the walls develop cracks. The man becomes distracted, irritable, emotionally withdrawn, not because he doesn't love his wife, but because maintaining two emotional lives is exhausting. He may start fights over nothing, not because he's angry at her, but because the stress of the double life needs an outlet. He may become sexually distant, not because he's not attracted to his wife, but because his sexual energy is being split. He may become unusually generous, buying gifts, planning dates, saying "I love you" more often than usual, not because his love has deepened, but because the guilt needs somewhere to go. These are the behavioral changes that often precede the discovery, and they're worth paying attention to. Not as proof of infidelity, but as signs that something inside your man is under enormous strain.

I've talked to DL men about this compartmentalization, and they describe it in remarkably similar terms. One man said it felt like being two different people who share the same body. Another said it was like having two tabs open in a browser, when one is active, the other is still there, running in the background, using up energy. A third described it as a weight he could feel physically: a tightness in his chest that was always there, sometimes faint, sometimes crushing, but never entirely gone. The stress of maintaining the double life takes a toll on the man's health, mental, emotional, and physical. Many DL men report anxiety, insomnia, depression, and a pervasive sense of exhaustion that they can't explain to anyone because the explanation would require revealing the cause.

For the woman at home, the irony is cruel: the man is suffering, but the suffering is self-inflicted, and the person most affected by his coping mechanism, the emotional withdrawal, the irritability, the distance, is you. You end up absorbing the fallout of a crisis you don't even know exists.

The Geography of Secrecy: Distance as a Tool

Geography is one of the most underappreciated tools in the DL man's operational toolkit. The principle is simple: the farther the secret life is from the public life, the safer it feels. And the men who pursue trans women and femboys often deliberately seek partners who live in different cities, far enough away that the two worlds will never accidentally collide, but close enough to visit with a plausible cover story.

The two-hour radius is the sweet spot. Close enough for a day trip or an overnight stay. Far enough that there's zero chance of running into someone from his regular life. A man in Atlanta might pursue someone in Macon or Augusta. A man in Chicago might connect with someone in Milwaukee or Indianapolis. A man in Dallas might find his partner in Houston or San Antonio. The geography provides a natural buffer: a moat around the secret life that makes accidental discovery almost impossible.

For men who travel for work, the geography expands dramatically. A man whose job takes him to different cities every week has potential partners in every city on his route. I've spoken with trans women who told me their DL partners had connections in three or four cities: a different woman in each one, none of them knowing about the others, all of them thinking they were the only secret. The road becomes a lover's lane that stretches across state lines.

For the woman at home, the geographic dimension means that the secret life may be literally invisible to her. She's never going to spot his car in the wrong parking lot because the parking lot is a hundred miles away. She's never going to run into the other woman at the grocery store because the other woman lives in a different city. The geographic separation creates a sense of safety for the DL man that makes the behavior feel sustainable, which is part of why these relationships can go on for years before being discovered.

The Escalation Pattern: How the Secret Life Grows

One of the most important things women need to understand about the DL secret life is that it rarely stays at the level where it began. There is an escalation pattern that is remarkably consistent across the stories I've collected, and it follows a predictable arc.

Stage one is curiosity. The man begins consuming content, social media posts, adult content, profile browsing on dating apps. He's not interacting. He's watching, scrolling, absorbing. This stage can last weeks, months, or even years. Some men stay at this stage indefinitely and never move beyond it.

Stage two is interaction. He starts engaging: following accounts, liking posts, saving photos, and eventually sending direct messages. The interaction is tentative at first, compliments, small talk, testing the waters. He's gauging the response, seeing if the person is receptive, and managing his own anxiety about what he's doing.

Stage three is the first encounter. This is the point of no return for most men. The first time he meets a trans woman or femboy in person, the attraction goes from digital to physical, from fantasy to reality. And once it becomes real, once he's touched someone, been intimate with someone, experienced the attraction in three dimensions rather than two: it becomes almost impossible to put back in the box.

Stage four is routine. The encounters become regular. The relationship develops a rhythm. Communication becomes daily. Financial flows begin. The secret life develops its own infrastructure: the burner phone, the cover stories, the geographic patterns we've discussed. At this stage, the man is no longer dabbling. He's committed.

Stage five is entrenchment. The secret life becomes a fundamental part of who the man is. He has reorganized his schedule, his finances, and his emotional energy to accommodate it. The relationship with the trans woman or femboy has its own history, its own inside jokes, its own shared experiences. Walking away from it would feel like a second divorce: a loss of something real, even if it was built on deception.

Understanding this escalation pattern is important because it tells you something about where your man might be when you discover the truth. If he's at stage two, browsing and messaging but hasn't met anyone in person, the conversation and the path forward look very different than if he's at stage five, embedded in a multi-year relationship with someone he's genuinely bonded with. The earlier the discovery, the more options you have. The later the discovery, the more complex the unraveling becomes.

Marcus's Escalation

Marcus, a thirty-seven-year-old IT manager in Phoenix, described his own escalation pattern with painful clarity. "It started with the Explore page. Just pictures. I told myself I was just looking. Then I started following accounts. Told myself it was harmless. Then I liked a few photos. Then I saved a few. Then I DM'd one girl, just a compliment, just 'You're beautiful.' She responded. We started talking. Within a month, I was driving to Tucson to meet her for dinner. Within three months, I was seeing her every two weeks. Within a year, I was in love. And at every single stage, I told myself I could stop anytime I wanted. That was the biggest lie I told, not to my wife, but to myself."

Marcus's wife discovered the truth at stage five. By then, the relationship was nearly two years old. "If she had caught me at stage one, when I was just looking at pictures, maybe we could have had a conversation. Maybe we could have worked through it. By the time she found out, I was in too deep. I had feelings for this person. I had made promises. Unwinding all of that wasn't just hard: it was like amputating a part of myself."

What the Community Knows: The Open Secret

Here's something I can tell you from my own experience in the LGBTQIA community: your man's secret is probably less secret than he thinks. Within the queer and trans community, DL men are discussed frequently, openly, and with a mixture of frustration, compassion, and pragmatism. Trans women and femboys talk to each other. They share stories. They compare notes. They warn each other about men who are known to be DL. In cities with active LGBTQIA communities, the names of DL men circulate through social networks like currency.

I have been in rooms, lounges, house parties, after-hours gatherings, where trans women pulled out their phones and showed each other the DMs they were receiving from married men. I have watched groups of femboys scroll through dating apps and point out which profiles belonged to men they knew were DL, "That's Sister So-and-So's husband," or "That's the deacon from such-and-such church." The community knows. The wives are the last to find out, not because the information doesn't exist, but because they don't have access to the social networks where the information circulates.

This is not about gossip or cruelty. It's about a community protecting itself. Trans women share information about DL men partly because some of these men can be dangerous, violent when they fear exposure, abusive when they feel cornered. Knowing who is DL and how they behave is, for trans women, a survival skill. But it also means that the DL man's carefully constructed secrecy has a massive blind spot: he may have successfully hidden his secret from his wife, his church, and his coworkers, but he hasn't hidden it from the community of people his partner belongs to.

For women, this community knowledge represents a strange paradox. The information about your man exists, it's out there, being discussed by people you'll probably never meet, in spaces you'll probably never enter. And while it's unlikely that someone from the trans community will come to you directly with the truth, it's not impossible. As I mentioned in Chapter 3, some trans women and femboys do eventually reach out to the wife, out of guilt, out of anger, or simply out of a sense that the woman at home deserves to know. When that happens, the secret life collapses all at once, in the most devastating way possible.

I've seen this play out in our community more times than I can count. A trans woman gets tired of being treated as a secret. She gets tired of the broken promises: the "I'm going to leave her eventually" that never materializes. She gets tired of holidays alone, weekends alone, watching him post family photos on his public Instagram while she sits in an apartment he pays for but will never visit on a Sunday. And one day, she decides she's done being hidden. She finds the wife's Facebook page. She sends a message. She attaches screenshots. And two women's lives are permanently changed by a single notification. The DL man's worst nightmare isn't his wife's detective skills. It's the moment the person he's been hiding decides she deserves to be visible too.

Patricia's Realization

Patricia is fifty-one and lives in Richmond, Virginia. When she discovered her husband Gregory's four-year relationship with a trans woman named Diamond who lived in Norfolk, about ninety minutes away, she said the geography was the part that enraged her most.

"Every other Saturday, he told me he was playing golf with his buddies in Virginia Beach," Patricia said. "Every other Saturday, for four years. That's over a hundred Saturdays. And I never questioned it. Never once. Because Virginia Beach is a normal place to play golf, and Gregory loves golf, and why would I think twice about it? But he wasn't playing golf. He was stopping in Norfolk on the way to the course, or instead of the course, and spending the afternoon with Diamond. Sometimes he'd actually play nine holes afterward so he'd come home smelling like grass and sunscreen. The man thought of everything."

Patricia's story illustrates how geography and cover stories work together to create what feels like an airtight system of deception. The ninety-minute drive. The plausible destination. The corroborating details. For four years, it worked perfectly. Until it didn't.

What You Do with This Information

I've given you a lot in this chapter: a detailed map of the secret life's infrastructure. And I know that reading it might have triggered recognition. Maybe you've seen some of these patterns in your own man. Maybe the cash withdrawals, the gym time, the second phone, the geographic excuses are suddenly clicking into place. Or maybe you haven't seen any of this, and you're here because you're trying to understand someone else's situation. Either way, the information is yours now.

But I want to leave you with a word of caution: this chapter is not a surveillance manual. I did not lay out these patterns so you could turn into a private investigator, checking his phone while he sleeps and tracking his Venmo transactions. That path leads to obsession, not healing. If you see patterns in your relationship that match what I've described, the answer is not to surveil harder. The answer is to have a conversation, with him, with a therapist, or with both, armed with the knowledge this book has given you.

Because knowledge is not the same as proof. And proof is not the same as resolution. What you ultimately need is not evidence of what he's doing, you may already have that, or you may find it soon enough. What you need is the clarity to decide what you're going to do about it. And that clarity comes not from catching him, but from understanding, deeply, honestly, and without illusion, what you're dealing with.

I also want to speak directly to the women who have read this chapter and recognized none of it, no second phone, no cash withdrawals, no suspicious gym sessions. That doesn't necessarily mean everything is fine, and it doesn't necessarily mean everything is wrong. What it means is that you don't have enough information yet to know either way. And the worst thing you can do is project the patterns from this chapter onto a man who may be completely faithful. This book is a tool, not a weapon. Use it to understand a situation you're already suspicious about, not to create suspicion where none existed before.

And for the women who have read this chapter and recognized everything, who are sitting right now with the sick feeling of certainty settling into their stomach, I want you to know that you are not alone. You are not the first woman to discover this. You will not be the last. And the chapters that follow are written specifically for you: to help you process the emotional devastation, to help you have the conversations that need to happen, and to help you find your way to whatever "forward" looks like for your life.

The next chapter takes us into the emotional dimension of these secret relationships, what happens when DL men don't just pursue trans women and femboys for physical attraction, but actually fall in love. Because when love enters the equation, everything changes. For him, for her, and for you. And if you thought the operational details were complicated, wait until you see what happens when the heart gets involved.

Nicole told me one last thing before we ended our conversation. She said: "The money I can get back. The time I can't. But the thing I needed most was what you're trying to give women in this book: the ability to see the machine. Once I could see how it worked, the phone, the apps, the cash, the gym excuse, all of it, it stopped being this big, terrifying mystery and started being a problem I could actually deal with. Seeing the machine took its power away."

That's what this chapter was for. Now you can see the machine. The apps, the aliases, the burner phones, the cash withdrawals, the gym excuses, the geographic buffers, the escalation from curiosity to commitment, the compartmentalization that lets him sleep next to you at night, and the community that knows his name even when you don't know theirs. It's a lot to take in. But seeing it clearly is the first step toward dealing with it effectively. And dealing with it effectively is the first step toward taking back the power that his secrecy stole from you.

Let's keep going.

CHAPTER SIX

The Emotional Connection: Why Some DL Men Fall in Love

This is the chapter most women don't want to read. And I understand that. Because everything up to this point, the psychology, the science, the apps, the money, can be processed at a distance. It's information. It's mechanics. It hurts, but it's the kind of hurt you can analyze. This chapter is different. This chapter is about the heart. And when the heart gets involved, the hurt goes to a different level entirely.

Because here is a truth that nobody wants to say out loud: some DL men who pursue trans women, femboys, and drag queens don't just have sex with them. They don't just date them. They fall in love with them. Real, genuine, deep-in-your-chest, up-at-three-in-the-morning, willing-to-risk-everything love. The kind of love that makes a man cry when he talks about it. The kind that makes him whisper "I love you" into a phone he hides under his car seat. The kind that makes him lie awake next to his wife imagining a life where he doesn't have to choose.

If that last paragraph made your stomach drop, I understand. Stay with me anyway. Because understanding this dimension of the DL dynamic is not about torturing you, it's about giving you the complete picture so you can make the most informed decisions possible about your life. And you can't make a fully informed decision if you're operating under the assumption that your man's secret involvement was just physical. For many women, it wasn't. And that changes everything.

Beyond the Hookup: When DL Relationships Become Real

In Chapter 3, we drew the distinction between the DL man who has quick, anonymous encounters with masculine men and the DL man who builds ongoing relationships with feminine-presenting individuals. In Chapter 5, we explored the operational mechanics of how those relationships are maintained. Now we need to go deeper, into the emotional architecture of those relationships. What do they actually feel like from the inside? What happens when a man who is living a lie finds himself experiencing something that feels more real than the life he shows the world?

The answer, based on my conversations with dozens of DL men and the trans women and femboys involved with them, is this: these relationships often develop the same emotional trajectory as any other romantic relationship. There is a honeymoon phase: the intoxicating early days of discovery, desire, and mutual fascination. There is a deepening phase, where the initial attraction evolves into genuine care, concern, and emotional interdependence. There is a commitment phase, where the man starts making promises, planning around the relationship, integrating it into the structure of his life. And in some cases, there is a love phase, where the man arrives at the startling, terrifying, unspeakable realization that he is in love with this person.

I want to be absolutely clear: I am not romanticizing this. The entire relationship is built on a foundation of lies, lies to the woman at home, and often lies to the partner as well, who may be told that the man is single or "in the process of leaving." The emotional depth of the relationship does not make it ethical. But it does make it real. And pretending it isn't real, pretending that your man was just satisfying a physical urge, may prevent you from understanding what you're actually dealing with.

Keith's Story

Keith is forty-nine years old and has been married for twenty-four years. He's a school principal in a mid-sized city in Georgia. Active in his community. Respected. The kind of man whose wife gets stopped at the grocery store by people who tell her how lucky she is. Keith contacted me because he'd been carrying a secret for six years and said he was "drowning in it."

Keith met a trans woman named Serena through Instagram when he was forty-three. What started as a DM complimenting a photo became a daily conversation, then nightly phone calls, then a first meeting at a restaurant an hour from his home. Within three months, Keith was in love. He didn't plan it. He didn't want it. But it happened.

"I need you to understand," Keith told me, his voice cracking, "I love my wife. I have loved her since we were twenty-two years old. She is the mother of my children, she is my best friend, and I would take a bullet for her. But I also love Serena. And those two truths existing at the same time inside of me is the most painful thing I have ever experienced."

Keith described his love for Serena in terms that are indistinguishable from how any man might describe falling in love with any woman. The way his heart raced when her name appeared on his screen. The way conversations lasted hours without a single lull. The way he noticed small things about her, the way she stirred her coffee, the way she tilted her head when she laughed, and found them all devastatingly beautiful. "This is not a fetish," he said firmly. "This is not a phase. This is love. Complicated, impossible, wrong-in-every-way-that-matters love. But love."

Why Emotional Affairs Hit Harder: What the Research Says

Research on infidelity has consistently shown that emotional affairs can be as devastating, or more devastating, than purely physical ones, particularly for women. A large-scale study with approximately sixty-four thousand participants found that women tend to experience greater distress over emotional infidelity than physical infidelity, while men tend to be more upset by sexual betrayal. This gender difference has been replicated across multiple studies and is well-established in the psychological literature.

The reason is rooted in what emotional infidelity represents. When a man has a purely physical encounter, quick, anonymous, meaningless, the betrayed woman can at least cling to the framework that it was "just sex." It's painful, but it can be compartmentalized. The man made a terrible choice, but his heart was never involved. The relationship at home, she can tell herself, was never truly threatened at its core.

But when a man falls in love with someone else, when he has given his emotional intimacy, his vulnerability, his deepest thoughts to another person: the betrayal reaches into the foundation of the relationship itself. It's no longer just about sex. It's about the fact that the person who was supposed to be your emotional partner, your confidant, your person, has shared that sacred space with someone else. The intimacy that was supposed to belong to the marriage has been given away. And that kind of betrayal is uniquely devastating because it threatens something deeper than the body. It threatens the bond.

Therapists who specialize in infidelity recovery have noted that emotional affairs are often harder to heal from precisely because the involved partner developed real feelings. A purely physical affair can sometimes be processed as a mistake: a lapse in judgment that can be addressed and moved past. An emotional affair represents something more persistent: a genuine connection with another human being that the man chose to nurture. It wasn't a moment of weakness. It was an ongoing decision, made day after day, to invest his heart in someone other than you.

Sandra's Story

Sandra is forty-three and lives in Houston. She discovered her husband Wendell's three-year relationship with a trans woman named Jade when Jade sent Sandra a Facebook message that included screenshots of their conversation history. Sandra described reading through those messages as the most painful experience of her life, not because of any sexual content, but because of the emotional content.

"He told her things he never told me," Sandra said. "Things about his childhood. Things about his fears. Things about what he wanted out of life. He was more emotionally open with her in those text messages than he had been with me in seventeen years of marriage. I read a message where he told her, 'You're the only person I can be completely myself with.' Do you know what that does to a wife? To read that? To realize that the man you've built your life around has found his 'real self' with someone else?"

Sandra's pain wasn't about the sex. She told me she could have dealt with physical infidelity. She'd dealt with it before, years earlier, when Wendell had a brief affair with a coworker. They went to counseling, they worked through it, they rebuilt. "But this was different," she said. "With the coworker, he told me it was just physical. And I believed him because the evidence supported it. With Jade, the evidence told a completely different story. He was in love. He had given her a part of himself that I didn't even know existed. And I don't know how to get past that."

Inside His Heart: What the Emotional Landscape Looks Like

I'm going to ask you to do something difficult right now: I'm going to ask you to try, for a few minutes, to see this from his perspective. Not to excuse him. Not to forgive him. But to understand him. Because understanding what he's feeling is part of understanding what you're dealing with.

The DL man who falls in love with a trans woman or femboy is experiencing something that most of our cultural frameworks have no language for. He is a man who loves his wife, and that love is real. He is also a man who loves someone else, and that love is also real. He is not choosing one over the other because, in his internal experience, the two loves occupy different spaces. His love for his wife is rooted in history, family, duty, companionship, and the life they've built together. His love for his partner is rooted in desire, emotional freedom, the intoxication of being fully seen, and the particular intensity that comes from a relationship conducted in secret.

The secrecy itself, paradoxically, intensifies the emotional connection. Research on forbidden love and the "Romeo and Juliet effect" has shown that external barriers to a relationship can amplify the feelings within it. When a relationship must be hidden, every stolen moment feels more precious. Every risk taken to see the other person is a proof of commitment. Every whispered "I love you" carries more weight because it was said against impossible odds. The secrecy creates a pressure cooker that concentrates the emotional experience in ways that a normal, public relationship never would.

This is why DL men who have fallen in love often describe their secret relationship as feeling more real, more raw, and more honest than their marriage, even though the entire relationship is built on dishonesty. The irony is painful and it's important: the man feels most honest with the person who represents his biggest lie.

Jerome and the Question of Honesty

Jerome is thirty-seven and lives in Detroit. His involvement with a femboy named Sky has lasted just over two years. Unlike many of the men in this book, Jerome didn't describe his situation with shame or regret. He described it with something closer to bewildered wonder.

"With my wife, I'm the man everybody expects me to be," Jerome told me. "I'm strong. I'm stoic. I'm the provider, the protector, the rock. I don't complain. I don't cry. I don't show weakness. That's what she married, and that's what I give her. But with Sky, I'm... everything else. I'm soft. I'm vulnerable. I laugh different. I talk different. I let my guard down completely. Sky sees parts of me that my wife has never seen because I was taught those parts aren't supposed to exist."

I asked Jerome why he couldn't show those parts to his wife. He was quiet for a long time. Then: "Because she fell in love with the strong version. And I'm terrified that if she sees the soft version, she'll stop loving me. With Sky, the soft version is the one that was loved first. I never had to pretend."

Jerome's story illuminates something critical about the emotional dimension of DL relationships: for many of these men, the secret relationship is the first place they've ever felt emotionally free. The rigid expectations of Black masculinity, be strong, don't show emotion, provide and protect, create a shell around these men that their wives may never see past, because the shell is precisely what the marriage was built on. The trans woman or femboy, who exists outside those expectations, becomes the one person with whom the man can drop the mask. And that emotional liberation is addictive in a way that has nothing to do with sex.

The Triangle of Pain: Three People, Three Heartbreaks

What makes this dynamic so tragic is that there are three people in pain, not two. The wife at home. The man in the middle. And the trans woman or femboy on the other side. And each of them is hurting in a different way.

The wife is hurting because her trust has been shattered, her identity as a wife has been destabilized, and she is facing a reality she was never prepared for. Her pain is the pain of betrayal compounded by confusion: not just "he cheated" but "he cheated with someone I didn't expect, in a way I don't understand, and he may actually be in love."

The man is hurting because he is trapped between two lives that both feel real but cannot coexist. His pain is the pain of fragmentation: being one person in one room and a different person in another, knowing that the truth would destroy at least one of the worlds he's built, and possibly both. He loves two people and is lying to both of them about the full picture.

And the trans woman or femboy is hurting because she is in love with a man who will never fully claim her. Her pain is the pain of being a secret: of knowing that the man who tells her she's beautiful, who takes her to dinner, who holds her at night, will never introduce her to his mother, will never post her on his public Instagram, will never stand beside her in the daylight. She is loved in the shadows, and no matter how deep the love feels, the shadows remind her every day that she is not enough to bring him into the light.

I've sat with all three corners of this triangle, and what strikes me most is how much each person's pain mirrors the others. The wife says, "He chose someone else over me." The trans woman says, "He chose his public life over me." And the man says, "I can't choose. That's the whole problem. I can't choose." The inability to choose is not a moral failing in the way most people want it to be. It's the product of a situation that our culture made no room for: a man whose heart is genuinely divided between two people he genuinely loves, in a world that says he has to pick one and pretend the other doesn't exist.

Tamara's Story

Tamara is fifty and lives in Columbus, Ohio. She discovered her husband Earl's emotional relationship with a trans woman named Simone after Earl was hospitalized for a stress-related cardiac event. While Earl was in the ICU, his burner phone, which Tamara didn't know existed, rang in his overnight bag. She answered it. The voice on the other end said, "Baby, are you okay? I saw you didn't text me good morning and I'm worried."

That phone call unraveled five years of secrets. Tamara read through the entire phone that night while Earl was sedated. She found thousands of messages. Love letters, essentially. Photographs of Simone, beautiful, feminine, soft-spoken in the voice notes Tamara played with shaking hands. Plans they'd made for a trip they never took. A message from Earl that said: "If I could live two lives, I would live one with you and one with her, and both would be complete."

"That message broke me," Tamara told me. "Not because it was about another woman. But because it was true. I could see it in the messages. He loved her. The way he wrote to her was... poetic. Tender. Open. He told her things about himself that I had to discover by accident over twenty-five years of marriage. He gave her the parts of himself that I had been begging for. And the thing that haunts me most is this: when I looked at those messages, I didn't just see a man cheating. I saw a man who was more alive in those conversations than I had seen him in years."

Tamara hasn't left Earl. They are in therapy. But she told me the thing she's struggling with most isn't the infidelity, it's the grief. "I'm grieving the marriage I thought I had. I'm grieving the emotional intimacy I thought we shared. And I'm grieving the version of my husband who apparently existed all along but only showed himself to someone else. That's a grief I don't have a name for."

Redefining What Love Means in This Context

One of the hardest things about this chapter is that it asks you to hold two contradictory truths at the same time: your man's love for the other person is real, and your man's love for you is also real. Most of our cultural narratives about love are built on exclusivity: the idea that real love can only be directed at one person at a time, and that if he loves someone else, his love for you must be fake. But the DL men I've spoken with describe something more complicated than that.

Their love for their wives is the love of partnership: shared history, shared children, shared sacrifice, shared identity. It is the love that comes from building a life together, weathering storms together, growing old together. It is stable, enduring, and rooted in commitment.

Their love for their trans or femboy partners is the love of liberation: emotional freedom, sexual authenticity, the intoxication of being fully seen. It is the love that comes from being accepted in the parts of yourself that you've hidden from everyone else. It is intense, fragile, and rooted in vulnerability.

These two loves are not interchangeable. One does not replace the other. And the man caught between them is not lying when he says he loves both: he is, in his own tormented way, telling the truth. Whether that truth is something you can live with is entirely your decision. But recognizing it as truth, rather than dismissing it as manipulation or delusion, is part of the process of understanding what you're dealing with.

Jade Speaks

Jade is the trans woman who was involved with Sandra's husband Wendell. After Sandra gave me permission to share her story, I reached out to Jade separately, and she agreed to share her perspective. What she told me was striking in it's emotional clarity.

"People assume I'm the villain," Jade said. "The homewrecker. The temptress who stole somebody's husband. But I was in love with him too. I didn't pursue a married man on purpose. He came to me. He pursued me. He told me he was separated. By the time I found out the truth, I was already in deep. And by then, I couldn't walk away because I loved him."

Jade described the emotional toll of being in a DL relationship with devastating honesty. "Christmas alone. Thanksgiving alone. His birthday, alone. Every holiday, every milestone, every moment that a couple should share together, I spent alone because he was with her. And every time he left my apartment to go home to his family, a little piece of me broke. I wanted to be angry at his wife, but I couldn't be. She didn't know about me. She was innocent. The only person I could be angry at was him, and I was too in love with him to be angry for long."

When I asked Jade why she eventually sent those screenshots to Sandra, she said: "Because I hit a wall. Three years of being hidden. Three years of 'I'm going to leave her eventually.' Three years of waiting for a man to choose me, knowing he never would. I didn't send those messages to hurt his wife. I sent them because I was drowning and I needed the situation to end, one way or another. I needed the lie to stop. Even if it meant losing him."

The Impossible Grief: Why This Discovery Hits Different

For the woman who discovers that her man wasn't just physically involved but emotionally invested, perhaps even in love, the grief is uniquely complicated. It's not just the grief of betrayal. It's the grief of realization: the realization that your marriage contained a void you didn't know existed. That your husband was sharing his most vulnerable self with someone else. That the emotional intimacy you thought belonged to the two of you was being given away.

Researchers who study infidelity-related trauma describe the discovery of emotional infidelity as producing symptoms similar to post-traumatic stress: intrusive thoughts, flashbacks, hypervigilance, insomnia, loss of appetite, and a pervasive sense that the world is no longer safe or predictable. These symptoms can persist for months or years after the discovery, and they are often more intense when the affair involved deep emotional connection rather than purely physical contact.

What makes this particular form of emotional affair even more complicated is the gender identity dimension. The wife isn't just processing "he fell in love with someone else." She's processing "he fell in love with a trans woman" or "he fell in love with a femboy." And that added layer triggers a cascade of additional questions: Does this mean he's gay? Does this mean he was never attracted to me? Does this mean our entire relationship was a lie? Was he thinking about her when he was with me? Is he capable of loving a woman like me, or does he need something I can't provide?

These questions are agonizing, and many of them don't have clean answers. As we discussed in earlier chapters, his attraction to a trans woman or femboy is rooted in femininity, which means his attraction to you was also real. His love for you was real. But his capacity for love extended beyond the boundaries you were both told to expect, and that extension, his ability to love femininity in forms that go beyond cisgender womanhood, is what created the space for Serena, for Jade, for Sky, for all the names and faces that represent the other side of this story.

How to Tell: Signs That His Involvement Is Emotional, Not Just Physical

Women often ask me: "How do I know if he's just having sex or if he's actually in love?" It's a critical question, because the answer determines the conversation you need to have and the kind of professional help you need to seek. While I'm not a therapist, and

I'd strongly encourage you to work with one, here are the patterns that distinguish a physical DL arrangement from an emotional one.

The communication volume is the biggest indicator. A man who is having quick physical encounters communicates minimally: a few messages to arrange the meeting, maybe a text afterward, and then silence until the next time. A man who is emotionally involved communicates constantly: good morning texts, midday check-ins, long evening conversations, voice notes, photos shared throughout the day. If you discover a communication record that reads like a relationship, not like a transaction, you're looking at emotional involvement.

The content of the communication matters as much as the volume. Messages that contain personal vulnerability, stories about his childhood, his fears, his dreams, his frustrations at work or at home, indicate that he has opened an emotional channel with this person. Messages that contain terms of endearment, baby, babe, my love, beautiful, indicate romantic attachment. Messages that reference shared experiences, "Remember when we…", indicate a relationship with history and depth.

The financial pattern also tells a story. A man who is physically involved might spend money sporadically: a hotel room here, a meal there. A man who is emotionally involved spends money consistently and generously: regular transfers, gifts for no occasion, contributions to the other person's living expenses. The financial pattern of an emotional affair looks like the financial pattern of someone who is taking care of a partner, because that's exactly what he's doing.

And finally, watch for emotional displacement at home. A man who is having physical encounters may come home and be perfectly attentive: the compartmentalization we discussed in Chapter 5 keeps the two worlds separate. But a man who is emotionally involved often comes home distracted, preoccupied, or emotionally unavailable. His mind is elsewhere because his heart is elsewhere. He may be physically present at the dinner table but mentally replaying a conversation he had that afternoon with someone you don't know exists.

The Masculinity Trap: Why Black Men in Particular Seek Emotional Freedom Elsewhere

I want to address something that has come up in nearly every conversation I've had with DL men for this book, because it goes to the heart of why these relationships become emotional and not just physical. And it's something that, as a Black person in the LGBTQIA community, I've been watching play out for my entire adult life.

Black masculinity, as it is constructed in our culture, is extraordinarily rigid. The expectations are clear and non-negotiable: be strong, be stoic, be the provider, be the protector, don't cry, don't show weakness, don't ask for help, and never, ever let anyone see you be soft. These expectations are reinforced at every level, family, church, community, media, and they create men who are functional on the outside and starving on the inside. Starving for emotional expression. Starving for the freedom to be vulnerable. Starving for a space where they can take off the armor and just be human.

Many of the DL men I've spoken with describe their marriages, however loving, as environments where the armor cannot come off. Not because their wives are cold or uncaring, but because the marriage itself was built on the foundation of that armored masculinity. The wife fell in love with the strong, stoic, unshakeable man. And the man is terrified that if he reveals the softer, more complex, more emotionally hungry person underneath, the wife will be repulsed. Or disappointed. Or both.

The trans woman or the femboy represents, for many of these men, the first person who has ever seen them without the armor. And that emotional nakedness, being truly seen, truly known, truly accepted in all of their complexity, is what transforms a physical attraction into an emotional bond. It's not that the trans woman or femboy is inherently better at providing emotional support than the wife. It's that the man has given himself permission to need emotional support in that relationship in a way he never has at home.

For the woman reading this, I know this is painful to hear. The idea that your husband found emotional freedom with someone else, that he was more vulnerable, more open, more himself with another person, is a wound that goes deeper than infidelity. It suggests that there was a part of your relationship that was always incomplete, and you didn't know it. But I want you to sit with this: the incompleteness was not your fault. It was the result of a cultural system that taught your man to be a wall instead of a window. And that system failed both of you.

What This Means for Your Decision

If you're reading this chapter because you've discovered that your man is emotionally involved, not just physically involved, with a trans woman or femboy, then the decision in front of you is more complex than a simple stay-or-leave binary. You are not just deciding whether to forgive a sexual indiscretion. You are deciding what to do about a man who has a genuine emotional bond with another person. And that bond doesn't disappear just because you found out about it.

Some women in this situation discover that their marriages can survive the revelation and even be strengthened by the honesty that follows. This is rare, but it happens, usually with the help of a skilled therapist who specializes in complex sexuality and infidelity. Other women discover that the emotional dimension is the one thing they cannot forgive: they could have survived a physical affair, but knowing their husband gave his heart to someone else is a bridge too far. Still others find themselves in a complicated middle ground where they don't want to leave but don't know how to stay, where the love they still feel for their husband coexists with a grief that won't resolve.

All of these responses are valid. None of them are wrong. And the chapters that follow, particularly the ones on deprogramming shame, protecting your health, and making your decision, are designed to support you no matter which path you choose.

What I do want you to take from this chapter is this: if the emotional dimension is present in your situation, don't ignore it. Don't minimize it. Don't tell yourself "it was just sex" when you know it wasn't. Acknowledge the full scope of what happened, because only then can you begin the full process of healing. A wound that isn't fully cleaned doesn't fully heal. And the emotional wound of discovering that your husband loved someone else is the deepest wound this situation can inflict.

I also want to say something to the women who are reading this and feeling an emotion they didn't expect: empathy. Empathy for Jade, sitting alone on Christmas. Empathy for Keith, trapped between two loves. Empathy for Serena, who is loved but can never be claimed. If you're feeling that empathy, don't fight it. It doesn't mean you're weak. It doesn't mean you're betraying yourself. It means you're human. And this situation, in all of it's impossibility, all of it's pain, all of it's tangled humanity, deserves to be met with humanity, not just anger.

The anger has its place. It will come, and when it comes, let it come. But let it sit alongside the understanding this book is building. Anger alone will burn your house down. Anger informed by understanding can help you rebuild.

Keith told me something at the end of our conversation that I've been turning over in my mind ever since. He said:

"The cruelest thing about this whole situation is that the love is real. If it were fake, if it were just lust, just a phase, just something I could switch off, it would be easier. For everyone. But it's not. I love my wife and I love Serena and I don't know how to exist in a world where both of those things are true. And I suspect my wife, if she ever finds out, will be destroyed not by the fact that I cheated, but by the fact that I loved."

He's probably right. And that's why this chapter needed to exist. Not to destroy you with the truth, but to arm you with it. Because the truth, even when it's the worst truth you've ever heard, is always, always better than the lie.

In the next chapter, we shift the focus entirely to you. We're going to talk about the warning signs, the practical, observable indicators that something may be going on, and how to trust your intuition when the evidence is still ambiguous. Because before you can decide what to do, you need to know what you're looking at. And sometimes, the hardest part isn't finding the truth. It's allowing yourself to see it.

CHAPTER SEVEN

What This Means for You: A Woman's Guide to Understanding the Signs

Up to this point, this book has been building your understanding. Now it's time to build your toolkit. This chapter is the most practical one in the book. It's written directly for you: the woman who suspects something, the woman who has found something, or the woman who just needs to know what to look for. No theory. No composite stories. Just clear, concrete guidance on the signs, the signals, and the steps.

But before we get into the specifics, I need to say something important: this chapter is a tool, not a weapon. The signs I'm about to describe are patterns, common behaviors observed across many situations. They are not guarantees. A man who suddenly starts going to the gym more often might be having an affair. He also might be going to the gym more often. A man who becomes protective of his phone might be hiding something. He also might just be a private person. Context matters. Your relationship matters. Your instincts matter. Use what follows as a lens to sharpen your vision, not as a verdict to convict your man before you've had a conversation.

That said, if you're reading this book, something brought you here. Something in your gut, in your observations, in the pattern of your life together made you pick this up. And I have learned, through years of being in community with women on every side of this situation, that a woman's intuition is almost never completely wrong. It might be wrong about the details. But the feeling, the sense that something is off, that feeling is almost always pointing at something real.

Behavioral Red Flags: Changes You Can See

The first category of signs is behavioral, things he does, or stops doing, that represent a departure from his established patterns. The key word is change. A man who has always gone to the gym five times a week is not a red flag. A man who suddenly starts going to the gym five times a week, after years of barely going at all, might be.

Changes in Grooming and Appearance

This is one of the most commonly reported early signs. A man who starts paying significantly more attention to his appearance, buying new clothes, trying new colognes, grooming more carefully, suddenly caring about his haircut, shaving body hair he never used to shave, is often doing so because he's trying to impress someone new. When that someone is a trans woman or femboy who invests heavily in her own presentation, the man often unconsciously raises his own grooming standard to match. He doesn't want to show up looking like he just rolled off the couch when she looks like she stepped out of a magazine.

Pay particular attention if his grooming changes happen on specific days or before specific outings. If he showers and puts on cologne before "going to Home Depot," that's worth noticing. If he changes his clothes before an "errand," that's worth noticing. If he suddenly has opinions about his wardrobe when he never did before, that's worth noticing.

There are also grooming changes that are specific to this dynamic rather than general infidelity. If your man starts paying attention to trans beauty content on social media, commenting on wigs or makeup in ways he never did before, or showing a new awareness of feminine presentation details, "That woman's lace front is laid" or "She has a nice set of nails", he may be revealing a vocabulary he acquired from spending time in spaces where those details are discussed. A man who can identify a lace front wig on sight didn't learn that from ESPN. He learned it from proximity to someone who wears them.

Changes in Schedule and Availability

As we covered in Chapter 5, time is the currency of the secret life. Look for new patterns that create blocks of unaccounted-for time. A new weekly commitment, a "men's group," a "poker night," a "standing meeting at work", that appeared out of nowhere. Business trips that became more frequent. Errands that now take twice as long as they used to. A gym routine that shifted from thirty minutes to two hours. An evening commute that used to take forty-five minutes but now regularly takes an hour and a half.

The common thread is the creation of time windows, regular, recurring blocks of time that are explained by a plausible but unverifiable cover story. The cover story is designed to be boring enough that you won't question it. Nobody interrogates a man about his gym session or his trip to the hardware store. That's the point.

Changes in Mood and Emotional Availability

A man who is living a double life is under constant stress, and that stress manifests in his emotional behavior at home. Common patterns include increased irritability, snapping at you or the kids over minor things, because the weight of the secret is compressing his patience. Emotional withdrawal, becoming quieter, more distant, less engaged in conversations, less interested in family activities.

Guilt-driven generosity, suddenly buying you flowers, planning a date night, telling you he loves you more often than usual, as if trying to compensate for the betrayal you don't yet know about. And unprovoked defensiveness, reacting aggressively to innocent questions about his day, his plans, or his whereabouts, as if any inquiry is an accusation.

One woman I spoke with described it perfectly: "It was like living with two different men. Some days he was the most attentive, loving husband in the world. Other days he was cold and distant and I couldn't figure out what I'd done wrong. I hadn't done anything wrong. His mood wasn't about me at all: it was about whatever was happening in his other life that I didn't know about."

New Interests in Trans or LGBTQ Culture

This is a sign that is specific to the dynamic we're discussing, and it's one that many women don't think to look for because it doesn't fit the traditional framework of infidelity. A man who begins showing unusual interest in LGBTQ content, transgender topics, or drag culture, watching drag competition shows with sudden enthusiasm, following trans influencers on social media, having opinions about gender identity issues he never cared about before, may be signaling an internal shift that has an external cause. This doesn't mean every man who watches a drag show is secretly DL. It does mean that a sudden, unexplained interest in a cultural space he previously had no connection to is worth paying attention to, especially if it appears alongside other signs on this list.

Digital Red Flags: The Phone Tells a Story

In the digital age, the phone is where the secret life lives. And the way a man handles his phone can tell you as much as what's actually on it.

Phone Behavior Changes

The most commonly reported digital red flag is a change in how he relates to his phone. A man who used to leave his phone on the kitchen counter without a second thought but now carries it with him everywhere, to the bathroom, to the garage, to bed, is guarding something. A man who used to hand you his phone casually when you needed to look something up but now hesitates, angles the screen away, or makes excuses is protecting something. A man whose phone suddenly has a new passcode, facial recognition, or fingerprint lock that he didn't have before has something he doesn't want you to see.

Watch also for the phone-face-down phenomenon. A man who consistently places his phone face-down on every surface is preventing notifications from being visible. This is such a common behavior among men with secret lives that trans women and femboys I've spoken with actually use it as a litmus test: "If he puts his phone face-down every time he sets it down, he's hiding something. Every time."

App and Browsing Patterns

If you do get access to his phone, here's what to look for. Dating apps are the obvious ones: Taimi, Butterfly, Translr, Transdr, Lex. But remember, many DL men use mainstream apps with trans-inclusive settings, so Tinder, Hinge, OkCupid, or Bumble could also be in play. Check for apps hidden in folders, many men create folders labeled "Utilities" or "Finance" and bury dating apps inside them. Check the App Store or Google Play for download history, even if the app has been deleted from the phone, it may still appear in the download log.

Browser history is another treasure trove, but savvy men know to use incognito or private browsing mode. If his browser history is suspiciously empty, no history at all for days or weeks, that itself is a sign. Nobody uses the internet without leaving any trace unless they're deliberately erasing their tracks. Check also for secondary browser apps, some men download browsers like Firefox Focus or DuckDuckGo specifically because they don't retain history by default.

Social media is perhaps the most revealing. Check his Instagram following list for accounts that are clearly trans women or femboys. Check his Twitter likes and retweets. Check his TikTok "for you" page if you can access it: the algorithm reveals what he's been watching and engaging with. And look for secondary accounts: a private Instagram with a different username, a Twitter handle that doesn't match any name you recognize. If he has multiple accounts on any platform, ask yourself why.

Victoria's Story

Victoria is thirty-two and lives in Charlotte. She found her husband Marcus's secret Instagram account by accident: she was logged into his phone to check their shared Amazon account and noticed Instagram was logged into two profiles.

"The second account had no profile picture and a random username, just letters and numbers," Victoria told me. "It was following over three hundred people. Every single one was a trans woman or a femboy. Beautiful, feminine, heavily followed accounts. And he wasn't just following them: he was in several of their DMs. Some of the conversations were months old. Some were active that week."

Victoria described the moment of discovery as a kind of slow-motion free fall. "I sat on the toilet lid and scrolled for forty-five minutes. And with every message I read, the man I thought I married became less recognizable. Not because he was attracted to trans women, I could eventually wrap my mind around that. But because he had built an entire digital life that I knew nothing about. He had a whole personality on that account, flirty, confident, forward, that I had never seen. He was a different man on that screen than the man who sat across from me at breakfast every morning."

Victoria's advice to other women: "Check for multiple account logins. On Instagram, it's right there in the settings. On Twitter, same thing. If he has a second account on any platform, and he hasn't told you about it, that's your answer right there. People don't have secret accounts for no reason."

Communication App Red Flags

Beyond dating apps and social media, look for communication apps that prioritize privacy. Telegram, Signal, and WhatsApp all offer disappearing messages, conversations that auto-delete after a set period. If your man has Telegram or Signal installed and you didn't know he used them, that's a question worth asking. Look also for the "archived" or "hidden" chat features in WhatsApp, which allow conversations to be stored out of the main chat list. And check for Google Voice or TextNow, apps that provide a second phone number without requiring a second phone, allowing a man to maintain an entire separate communication channel on the same device.

Financial Red Flags: Follow the Money

We covered the financial architecture in Chapter 5, but it bears repeating in this practical context. The financial signs that specifically suggest involvement with a trans woman or femboy, as opposed to general infidelity, include regular, predictable payments through Venmo, CashApp, or Zelle to a name or username you don't recognize. These payments often have no memo or a vague one like a single emoji. They tend to be in round numbers, fifty, a hundred, two hundred, and occur on a consistent schedule.

Look for cash withdrawals that form a pattern. ATM withdrawals every Friday, or on the days he has his "standing meeting." Larger-than-usual cash-back amounts at the grocery store or gas station. Credit card charges at stores that don't align with your household, beauty supply stores, wig shops, lingerie retailers, upscale restaurants you've never been to together. Hotel charges in cities that don't match his stated travel. Gas charges that suggest he's driving farther than he claims, if the gas station receipt is from a town an hour away but he said he was at the office, the math doesn't work.

And pay attention to the emergence of financial secrecy. A man who was always open about finances but now redirects statements to a new email, opens a credit card you don't know about, or becomes defensive when you ask about a charge has something to hide. Financial transparency in a marriage is a baseline of trust. When that transparency erodes, the trust is already under attack.

Sexual Red Flags: Changes in the Bedroom

This is a sensitive area, but it's one that women frequently identify as one of the earliest signs that something had changed.

Sexual behavior in a relationship exists on a spectrum that is unique to every couple, and changes in that spectrum can signal a range of things, stress, aging, health issues, medication side effects. But certain changes, particularly in combination with other signs on this list, can indicate that your man's sexual energy is being directed elsewhere.

A decrease in sexual frequency or interest is the most obvious sign. If a man who was consistently interested in sex suddenly loses interest; or if the frequency drops significantly without an obvious explanation like health problems or major life stress, it may be because his sexual appetite is being satisfied elsewhere. This is particularly telling if the decrease coincides with other changes: new gym habits, more phone privacy, unexplained absences.

Conversely, some women report an increase in sexual attention from their husbands around the time the affair began. This can be guilt-driven: the man overcompensates sexually at home to assuage his conscience or to preemptively deflect suspicion. If sex suddenly feels performative, more like he's proving something than connecting with you, that shift in energy is worth noting.

The most specific indicator, and the one that women in this particular situation report most often, is a change in what he wants in the bedroom. New requests. New positions. New interests that seem to have appeared from nowhere. If your man suddenly introduces preferences or techniques he's never expressed before, the question of where he learned them or what inspired them is a fair one. People's sexual interests evolve naturally over time, but sudden, specific changes that coincide with other red flags may not be a coincidence.

Renee's Story

Renee is forty-four and lives in Memphis. She said the first thing that triggered her suspicion wasn't his phone or his schedule: it was the sex.

"Our sex life had been good for twenty years," Renee told me. "Consistent, comfortable, satisfying. And then, over the course of maybe six months, everything changed. He wanted things he'd never wanted before. He was more aggressive. He was more… specific about what he wanted me to wear, how he wanted me to look. He wanted me in longer wigs. Longer nails. More makeup. He started commenting on my outfits in ways he never had, always pushing me toward more feminine, more done-up. And I thought, 'Where is this coming from?'"

The answer, Renee later discovered, was a trans woman named Celeste whom her husband had been seeing for over a year. "He was trying to make me into her," Renee said quietly. "The wigs, the nails, the makeup: he was trying to get from me what he was getting from her. And when I couldn't be that, because I'm not that, because I'm me, his frustration started showing. That's when I knew something was deeply wrong."

One final note on sexual red flags: if your partner suggests or insists on STI testing when it was never part of your routine, pay attention. A man who suddenly wants to "get checked" or who becomes unusually interested in sexual health discussions may be managing a risk he knows about and you don't. Conversely, a man who resists testing when you suggest it may be afraid of what the results would reveal, not just medically, but in terms of the questions that would follow. And if condom wrappers appear in his car, his bag, or his pockets when your relationship doesn't involve condom use, the explanation is obvious. We'll discuss the health dimension in much greater detail in Chapter 9.

Trusting Your Intuition: The Sign That Has No Name

I have saved this section for last because, in many ways, it is the most important. Every woman I've spoken with who has been through this experience has said some version of the same thing: "I knew. Before I found the phone. Before I saw the charges. Before I found the app. I knew. I just didn't want to believe it."

Female intuition is not magic. It's pattern recognition. It's your brain processing thousands of micro-signals: the way he looked at his phone, the half-second pause before he answered a question, the slight shift in his energy when he came home, the kiss that felt a little too performative; and assembling them into a feeling that something is wrong. That feeling is data. It's imprecise data, and it can be wrong about the specifics. But the feeling itself, the alarm bell ringing in the back of your mind, deserves to be respected.

I am not telling you to act on intuition alone. I am telling you not to dismiss it. If something feels off, honor that feeling by paying closer attention. Not by becoming paranoid. Not by reading into every innocent text message. But by allowing yourself to see clearly instead of talking yourself out of what your gut is trying to tell you. The women who discovered the truth earliest were the ones who listened to their intuition. The women who discovered it latest were the ones who spent years telling themselves, "I'm just being crazy." You're not crazy. You might be right.

Keisha's Story

Keisha is twenty-nine and lives in Baltimore. She is the youngest woman I interviewed for this book, and her story illustrates how the DL dynamic is evolving in the social media generation.

Keisha's boyfriend Darius didn't have a burner phone or a secret credit card. He wasn't old enough or established enough for those kinds of operational layers. His secret life existed entirely on his primary phone, hidden behind app locks and private browsing, and Keisha discovered it through a combination of intuition and a single unlucky notification.

"His phone lit up while he was in the shower," Keisha told me. "A Telegram notification from someone with a butterfly emoji as their name. The preview said, 'Can't wait to see you tomorrow.' That was it. One notification. But I knew. I didn't know the specifics yet, but I knew. Because Darius had never mentioned using Telegram, and nobody I knew used butterfly emojis like that."

It took Keisha two weeks of quiet observation before she found enough to confront Darius. In those two weeks, she paid attention to everything: which days he came home later than usual, when he was most protective of his phone, how his energy shifted on the days he said he was "hanging with the boys." When she finally saw his Telegram open for a split second while he was showing her a video, she saw enough, a string of messages with photos exchanged, pet names, plans to meet, to know the truth.

The person Darius was talking to was a twenty-three-year-old femboy named Rio. "I wasn't angry at Rio," Keisha said. "Rio didn't owe me anything. I was angry at Darius for looking me in my face every day and acting like everything was fine. And I was angry at myself for ignoring the feeling in my gut for as long as I did. That Telegram notification wasn't the first sign. It was the tenth. It was just the first one I couldn't explain away."

Denise's Story

Denise is thirty-eight and lives in Nashville. She discovered her husband Corey's involvement with a trans woman not through his phone, not through his finances, and not through a third party. She discovered it through a feeling she couldn't shake.

"Nothing specific was wrong," Denise told me. "I couldn't have pointed to a single thing and said, 'That. That right there.' It was more like... a vibration. Like the frequency of our relationship had shifted and I could feel it in my body but I couldn't name it. He was still loving. Still attentive. Still came home on time, still called me during the day. But something was... off. Like he was playing a role he used to live naturally."

Denise sat with that feeling for almost a year before she found evidence. When she finally did, a second Instagram account she stumbled across by accident, she said the predominant emotion wasn't shock. It was relief. "I wasn't crazy. The feeling was real. Something was wrong, and now I knew what it was. The truth was devastating, but the not-knowing was worse. At least now I could deal with reality instead of fighting my own perception."

What Not to Do When You First Discover the Truth

If you are reading this chapter because you've already found something, or because you're about to go looking, I need to give you some guidance about what not to do in the immediate aftermath of discovery. Because what you do in the first forty-eight hours can significantly impact your options going forward.

Do not confront him in a state of emotional crisis. The discovery triggers a flood of adrenaline, rage, grief, and disbelief. If you confront him while you're in the grip of those emotions, the conversation will not be productive. He will become defensive. You will become accusatory. The conversation will devolve into shouting, denial, and mutual devastation. Give yourself at least twenty-four to forty-eight hours to sit with the information before you decide how and when to have the conversation.

Do not destroy the evidence. Your first impulse might be to delete everything, throw the phone, burn the pictures. Don't. The evidence is your leverage and your clarity. Screenshot everything. Save it somewhere he cannot access, your own cloud storage, a trusted friend's email, a flash drive. You may need it later, for the conversation, for therapy, for legal purposes if it comes to that.

Do not broadcast it immediately. The urge to call your mother, your sister, your best friend, to tell someone, anyone, because the weight of the secret is crushing you, is completely understandable. But be strategic about who you tell and when. Once you tell someone, you cannot untell them. Their reaction will influence your decision-making at a time when you need to think clearly. Choose one trusted, emotionally stable person to confide in. Save the larger conversation for after you've had time to process.

Do not contact the other person. I know this is hard. Every fiber of your being may want to reach out to the trans woman or femboy, to confront her, to demand answers, to see who she is up close. Resist that urge, at least initially. Contacting the other person before you've talked to your man puts you in a reactive position and gives him time to construct a defense. It also puts you in a potentially volatile emotional exchange with someone who may be just as hurt and just as angry as you are. Let the first conversation be between you and him.

Do not make any permanent decisions. Don't file for divorce. Don't change the locks. Don't empty the bank account. Don't post on social media. In the immediate aftermath of discovery, your judgment is compromised by trauma. Every major decision should wait until you've had time to process, preferably with the support of a therapist who understands this specific dynamic. The decisions you make in the first week are almost never the decisions you'd make a month later when the initial shock has passed.

What to Do: First Steps Forward

Now that I've told you what not to do, here's what you should do.

Secure the evidence. Quietly, calmly, systematically. Screenshots, photos of the phone screen, bank statements printed or saved digitally. Store it all somewhere safe.

Find a therapist. Not next month. This week. And not just any therapist, one who has experience with infidelity, complex sexuality, and ideally, LGBTQ-affirming care. You need someone who won't respond to your situation with shock or judgment, because you're already dealing with enough of both. You need someone who can help you process the layers of this discovery: the infidelity layer, the sexuality layer, the identity layer, and the grief layer that sits underneath all of them.

Take care of your body. Trauma lives in the body. You may not be eating, sleeping, or functioning normally. Force yourself to eat something. Force yourself to rest, even if you can't sleep. Drink water. Move your body, walk, stretch, breathe. Your brain cannot make good decisions if your body is in crisis mode.

When you are ready, and only when you are ready, have the conversation. Come to it prepared: know what you've found, know what questions you need answered, and know what outcome you're hoping for. The conversation doesn't have to happen all at once. It can happen in stages. But it does have to happen, because silence is the soil the secret life grows in, and you have the power to end the silence on your terms.

How to Approach the Conversation

When you are ready to have the conversation, preparation is your greatest ally. The goal of the first conversation is not to resolve everything. It's not to decide the future of your marriage. It's not even to get him to admit everything. The goal of the first conversation is to break the silence, to let him know that you know, and to begin the process of bringing truth into a relationship that has been operating on lies.

Choose the time and place carefully. Not when the kids are home. Not when either of you has somewhere to be in an hour. Not in a public space. You need privacy, time, and enough physical safety to have an honest conversation. Some women choose to have the conversation in the presence of a therapist: a controlled environment where a professional can manage the emotional temperature. If that's an option, it's a good one.

Lead with what you know, not what you suspect. Present the evidence calmly. "I found this." "I saw this." "This is what I know." Don't ask him to confess: that gives him the opportunity to deny, deflect, and minimize. State what you've found and let him respond. His response will tell you a great deal about where he is emotionally: a man who collapses into tears and confession is in a very different place than a man who becomes hostile and accusatory.

Be prepared for denial. Most men, regardless of the evidence, will deny in the first conversation. Some will deny even when confronted with screenshots. This is not necessarily malicious, it's panic. The life he has built, the identity he has maintained, the wall between his two worlds, all of it is crumbling in real time, and denial is the last brick in that wall. Don't let his denial shake your confidence in what you know. You didn't imagine it. The evidence is real. And the truth will come out eventually, even if it doesn't come out in the first conversation.

Be prepared also for the conversation to include things you weren't expecting. He may reveal a longer history than you knew. He may reveal additional partners. He may reveal feelings and desires that he has been hiding for his entire adult life. The conversation, once started, can take turns you didn't anticipate. Let it. You don't have to resolve everything tonight. You just have to start.

Some women choose to write a letter instead of having a face-to-face conversation first. A letter gives you complete control over what you say and how you say it. It removes the possibility of being interrupted, shouted down, or thrown off by his emotional reaction. It also gives him time to absorb the information before responding, which can lead to a more honest and less reactive conversation when you do sit down together. There is no single right way to break the silence. There is only the way that gives you the most control and the most safety. Choose that way.

And finally: take care of yourself during and after the conversation. If you need to stop and come back tomorrow, stop. If you need to cry, cry. If you need to leave the room and breathe, leave. Your emotional well-being is not secondary to the conversation. It is the most important thing in the room.

The Stigma Barrier: Why This Discovery Is Harder to Talk About

There is a reason this chapter exists in a book and not in a magazine article or a support group handout. And that reason is stigma. The discovery that your partner has been involved with a trans woman or femboy carries a specific kind of social stigma that makes it qualitatively different from discovering a "regular" affair. And that stigma affects everything: who you tell, when you tell, and whether you tell at all.

Many women in this situation report feeling profoundly isolated, unable to confide in the people they would normally turn to for support. They can't tell their mother, because the conversation would require explaining what a trans woman is and watching their mother's face cycle through confusion, shock, and disgust. They can't tell their best friend, because they're terrified of being pitied, gossiped about, or secretly laughed at. They can't tell their pastor, because the church often treats this specific type of infidelity as uniquely shameful, worse than cheating with another woman, contaminated by associations with homosexuality and perversion that make the conversation toxic before it even begins.

I've sat with women who carried this secret for months, sometimes years, because the stigma of the discovery felt worse than the discovery itself. They chose to suffer in silence rather than risk the judgment of their community. And that silence is exactly what the DL dynamic depends on. The same cultural shame that keeps him in the closet keeps you in the closet. You both end up trapped in the same prison of secrecy, for different reasons but with the same result: isolation, silence, and pain that has no outlet.

If you are in this situation, I want to tell you something clearly: you have nothing to be ashamed of. His choices are not your shame. His desires are not your failure. The fact that the person he was involved with happened to be transgender does not make your situation more humiliating than any other infidelity: it just makes it more complicated. And you deserve support that meets the complexity of what you're going through, not judgment that adds to your burden.

Seek out a therapist who is both infidelity-informed and LGBTQ-affirming. If you cannot find one locally, telehealth options have expanded dramatically. Online support communities for women dealing with partner sexuality issues exist, and while you should be cautious about sharing personal details in any online space, knowing that other women have been through this, and survived it, can be a lifeline during the darkest days.

You do not have to navigate this alone. And you should not have to navigate it in silence. The stigma is real, but it is not more powerful than your need for support. Find your people, even if it's one person, and let them in.

This chapter gave you the signs. The previous chapters gave you the context. Together, they give you something that every woman in this situation desperately needs: the ability to see clearly. Not through the fog of denial. Not through the distortion of shame. Clearly. And clarity, as painful as it is, is always the beginning of power. You now know what to look for, in his behavior, in his phone, in his finances, in the bedroom, and in your own body's response to the shift in your relationship's frequency. You know how to protect evidence, how to find support, and how to approach the hardest conversation of your life. You are more prepared right now than you were when you opened this book. And that preparation is not just knowledge. It's armor.

The next chapter is going to take care of you. It's called "It's Not About You," and it's about deprogramming the shame and self-blame that women in this situation almost always carry. Because the signs we discussed in this chapter point to something he did. Not something you caused. Not something you deserved. Not something that reflects your worth as a woman, a wife, or a human being. The next chapter is going to make sure you know that, not just intellectually, but in your bones.

Before you turn that page, I want to speak to you one more time as someone who has been in the rooms where all of this plays out. I have watched women crumble under the weight of this discovery. I have also watched women put themselves back together, piece by piece, with a strength that humbled me. The women who made it through were not the ones who were the toughest or the angriest or the most prepared. They were the ones who were willing to see the truth, feel the pain, and then, after the tears, after the sleepless nights, after the questions that had no good answers, decide that their own life was worth fighting for. That's the decision this chapter is preparing you to make.

You may not feel ready. That's okay. You don't have to be ready today. You just have to be willing to keep reading, keep learning, and keep building the understanding that will eventually become your armor. Because when the time comes to act, and it will come, whether you initiate it or it arrives on its own, you will want to act from a place of knowledge, not ignorance. From clarity, not confusion. From power, not panic.

This chapter gave you the signs. The next chapters give you the strength. Let's keep going.

CHAPTER EIGHT

It's Not About You: Deprogramming Shame and Self-Blame

I want you to read the title of this chapter one more time. It's not about you. Say it out loud if you need to. Write it on a sticky note and put it on your bathroom mirror. Tattoo it on the inside of your eyelids if that's what it takes. Because if there is one message in this entire book that has the power to save your sanity, it's this one: what your man did, what he's attracted to, what he hid, and who he hid it with, none of that is a reflection of your worth, your beauty, your femininity, or your value as a woman. None of it.

And yet, I know that knowing this intellectually and believing it emotionally are two entirely different things. Every woman I've spoken with who has been through this experience has described the same devastating internal monologue: Was I not enough? Was I not pretty enough? Not feminine enough? Not sexy enough? Was there something wrong with me that made him need this? Could I have prevented it if I'd been more attentive, more adventurous, more... something?

No. The answer to every single one of those questions is no. And this chapter is going to explain why, not with platitudes or motivational slogans, but with the same honesty and depth that has carried us through the rest of this book. By the time you finish this chapter, I want the shame to be lighter. Not gone, I'm not naïve enough to think one chapter can undo years of cultural programming and weeks or months of emotional trauma. But lighter. Because you cannot begin to heal until you set down the weight that doesn't belong to you.

The Lies You Tell Yourself: Dismantling the Self-Blame Narratives

"If I Were More Feminine, He Wouldn't Have Needed This"

This is the most common lie, and the most destructive. The logic goes like this: he's attracted to hyper-feminine trans women and femboys, which means my femininity wasn't enough, which means I failed as a woman. Let me take that apart piece by piece.

First, as we established in Chapter 2, his attraction to heightened femininity is a feature of his psychology, not a deficit in yours. The research from Northwestern University showed that men attracted to trans women exhibit arousal patterns consistent with heterosexual attraction: they respond to femininity across a broader range of presentations than most men. This is about the breadth of his attraction spectrum, not the inadequacy of yours. You didn't fail to be feminine enough. He has a capacity for attraction that extends beyond what the culture prepared either of you to expect.

Second, the trans women and femboys who attract DL men invest enormous resources in achieving a level of femininity that is deliberately heightened, as we discussed in Chapter 4. You are not failing to compete with something natural. You are being compared, by your own tortured inner voice, not by reality, to a presentation that requires thousands of dollars, hundreds of hours, and a level of deliberate construction that has nothing to do with how women naturally exist in the world. Comparing your everyday femininity to a curated, amplified presentation is like comparing your home cooking to a five-star restaurant and concluding you don't know how to feed people. The comparison itself is the problem.

"I Should Have Known"

This lie is particularly cruel because it transforms you from a victim of deception into an accomplice to your own betrayal. If I should have known, then I'm partly responsible for not knowing. If I'm partly responsible, then I share the blame. And if I share the blame, then the devastation I'm feeling is somehow my fault.

Stop. You should not have known. You could not have known. The DL men described in this book are not casual liars. They are architects of deception who built elaborate systems specifically designed to prevent you from knowing: burner phones, hidden apps, secondary accounts, geographic buffers, compartmentalized emotional lives. You were not dealing with a man who left clues out of carelessness. You were dealing with a man who spent years engineering your ignorance. The fact that his system worked is not evidence of your naïveté. It's evidence of his commitment to the lie.

Research on betrayal trauma confirms that self-blame is one of the most common responses to discovering infidelity. Psychologists have found that betrayed partners frequently blame themselves as a way to maintain a sense of control: if I can figure out what I did wrong, I can prevent it from happening again. But this is an illusion. You didn't do anything wrong. The control you're seeking doesn't exist; because the decision to deceive was his, and his alone.

"Other Women Will Think Less of Me"

This lie is about social shame: the fear that if other people find out what your man was doing, they will pity you, judge you, or secretly believe something is wrong with you. This fear is especially intense in this specific situation because of the gender identity dimension. In a "regular" affair, the social script is at least somewhat familiar: your man cheated, you're the wronged wife, people rally around you. When the affair involves a trans woman or femboy, the script breaks down. People don't know how to react. Some will express sympathy but secretly treat the situation as gossip-worthy. Others will distance themselves because they don't understand and don't want to. And some, let's be honest, will quietly wonder what's wrong with you for being with a man like that.

I'm not going to tell you these reactions don't happen, because they do. I've seen them. I've watched women lose friendships over this, not because they did anything wrong, but because the people around them couldn't handle the complexity of the situation. But I am going to tell you this: the reactions of others are about their limitations, not yours. The person who pities you is projecting their own fear. The person who judges you is protecting their own denial. And the person who gossips about you is using your pain as entertainment because they don't have the emotional depth to sit with it as reality.

You do not owe anyone an explanation. You do not owe anyone your story. You get to choose who knows, what they know, and when they know it. And the people who deserve a place in your healing are the ones who respond to your truth with compassion, not curiosity.

"He Must Be Gay, and Our Whole Relationship Was a Lie"

We covered this extensively in Chapter 2, but it bears repeating here because this belief is at the root of so much unnecessary suffering. If he's gay, the logic goes, then he was never really attracted to me, which means our relationship was a performance, which means everything, the love, the sex, the children, the years, was fake.

It wasn't fake. As the Northwestern research demonstrated, men who are attracted to trans women show arousal patterns that are heterosexual in nature. Their attraction to femininity is genuine, and that attraction includes you. Your man was not performing desire for you. He desired you. He also desired someone else, someone whose femininity exists in a form that our culture doesn't have a comfortable category for. Both desires are real. And the fact that both exist does not cancel either one out.

Your relationship was real. The love was real. The intimacy was real. The betrayal was also real. All of these things coexist, and the pain of this situation is precisely that they all coexist: that something can be simultaneously true and built on a lie. Holding that contradiction is agonizing. But resolving it by telling yourself the whole thing was fake is a shortcut to a conclusion that isn't supported by the evidence, and it adds a layer of grief that you don't need to carry.

"I'm in Competition with a Trans Woman and I'm Losing"

This lie reframes your entire situation as a contest; and one you're destined to lose. If your man is attracted to someone who is arguably "more feminine" than you, the logic goes, then you are in a beauty pageant you didn't enter and can't win. This framing is toxic because it does two things simultaneously: it reduces your value to your appearance, and it positions the trans woman or femboy as your enemy.

You are not in a competition. You are in a marriage that was violated by dishonesty. The trans woman or femboy your man was involved with is not your rival: she is another person affected by his choices. As Carmen said in Chapter 4 and Jade said in Chapter 6, the women on the other side of this dynamic are often dealing with their own pain, their own isolation, and their own grief at being hidden. Turning them into your enemy might feel satisfying in the short term, but it doesn't serve your healing. The person who owes you answers, accountability, and truth is your man. He is the one who made promises to you. He is the one who broke them. Redirect your energy accordingly.

And as for the "losing" part of this lie: you cannot lose a contest that doesn't exist. Your worth as a woman, a wife, and a human being is not determined by comparison to anyone else, not a cisgender woman, not a trans woman, not a femboy, not a supermodel on a magazine cover. Your worth is inherent. It was there before him, it's there during this crisis, and it will be there after. The shame is trying to make you forget that. Don't let it.

Lynn's Turning Point

Lynn is forty-two and lives in Raleigh, North Carolina. Her turning point came seven months after discovery, in a therapy session she almost didn't attend.

"My therapist asked me to describe myself without mentioning my husband, my marriage, or what happened," Lynn told me. "And I couldn't do it. I opened my mouth and nothing came out. I had spent seven months so consumed by what he did that I had completely lost myself. I couldn't remember who I was before the discovery. My entire identity had been swallowed by his betrayal."

Lynn's therapist gave her an assignment: spend one week writing down one thing each day that was true about her that had nothing to do with her husband. By the end of the week, she had a list: she was a good mother, a talented cook, a dedicated teacher, a loyal friend, a woman who could make anyone laugh, a woman who had run a half-marathon at thirty-nine, a woman who had survived things harder than this before.

"That list became my anchor," Lynn said. "Every time the shame tried to swallow me, I went back to that list. I am these things. These things are mine. No man's choices can take them from me. And slowly, the shame started losing its grip."

Francine's Story

Francine is fifty-five and lives in St. Louis. She discovered her husband Robert's involvement with a trans woman eight years ago and has spent those eight years in therapy, working through every dimension of the betrayal. She stayed in the marriage. She and I spoke about the shame specifically.

"The shame almost killed me," Francine said, and she wasn't being dramatic. "I stopped eating. I stopped sleeping. I stopped leaving the house. I was convinced that if I went to the grocery store, everyone would look at me and know. Know that my husband preferred a trans woman to me. Know that I was the kind of woman whose man wanted something she couldn't provide. The shame was physical. I felt it in my chest, in my stomach, in my skin. I felt dirty. I felt broken. I felt like the least desirable woman on the planet."

Francine's therapist, who specialized in betrayal trauma and was LGBTQ-affirming, helped her separate the threads of her pain. "She helped me understand that I was carrying three different kinds of shame, and I needed to deal with each one separately. The first was the shame of being cheated on, which is universal, which every woman who's been through infidelity carries. The second was the shame of the gender identity element: the specific stigma of my husband being with a trans woman, which made me feel like my situation was freakish, abnormal, something I couldn't talk about. And the third was the deepest: the shame of believing I was inadequate. That I lacked something fundamental. That my womanhood wasn't enough."

It took Francine two years to dismantle that third layer of shame. "My therapist told me something I will never forget. She said: 'Francine, you are not inadequate. Your husband's capacity for attraction is wider than average. That's about him. Your womanhood is complete. Your femininity is whole. You are not missing a piece. He has an extra piece that nobody prepared either of you for.' That reframing, from 'I'm lacking' to 'he has something extra', changed my entire relationship with the situation."

Understanding Betrayal Trauma: What's Happening Inside You

What you are experiencing has a name: betrayal trauma. It's not just sadness. It's not just anger. It's a specific form of psychological injury that occurs when someone you depend on for safety and stability violates your trust in a fundamental way. And the symptoms of betrayal trauma can be as severe and debilitating as the symptoms of any other form of trauma.

Researchers have documented that betrayal trauma can produce intrusive thoughts: the relentless mental replaying of the discovery, the images you found, the messages you read. Flashbacks, sudden, involuntary recollections of the moment you found out, triggered by sounds, smells, or situations that remind you of that day. Hypervigilance: the constant scanning of your environment for threats, the inability to relax, the sense that you must always be on guard. Insomnia, your mind refusing to quiet itself, replaying the evidence at three in the morning. Loss of appetite. Difficulty concentrating. Mood swings that make you feel like you're losing your mind.

These symptoms are not signs that you are weak, unstable, or overreacting. They are the normal neurological response to having your sense of safety shattered. Your brain is doing exactly what it's designed to do when it perceives a threat: mobilizing every resource to protect you. The problem is that the threat is not external, it's embedded in the most intimate relationship in your life, which means your brain cannot resolve it by fighting or fleeing. And that unresolvable state of alarm is what produces the symptoms that feel, to you, like you're falling apart.

You are not falling apart. You are having a normal reaction to an abnormal situation. And recognizing that, naming what's happening to you as trauma, not weakness, is the first step toward healing.

Michelle's Story

Michelle is thirty-nine and lives in Oakland. She is a nurse, and she told me that her professional understanding of trauma made her own experience both easier and harder to process.

"I recognized the symptoms immediately," Michelle said. "The hypervigilance, the insomnia, the intrusive thoughts, I see these in patients every day. I knew exactly what was happening to me clinically. But knowing didn't make it hurt less. If anything, it made me angrier, because I could see exactly how much damage he had done to my nervous system. I was walking around in a state of fight-or-flight for weeks. My cortisol levels were through the roof. I lost twelve pounds in three weeks because I couldn't eat. My hair started thinning. My body was in crisis because my brain believed I was under attack; and in a very real sense, I was."

Michelle's experience illustrates an important point: the physical toll of betrayal trauma is not imaginary. Research has documented that individuals who experience partner infidelity can develop somatic symptoms including weight loss, insomnia, difficulty concentrating, and loss of appetite. These are not just emotional responses: they are physiological responses, mediated by stress hormones, that affect the body as surely as any physical injury.

The Double Stigma: Why This Type of Betrayal Is Harder to Process

As we touched on in the previous chapter, the stigma surrounding this specific type of betrayal is different from, and often more isolating than, the stigma of a conventional affair. And that stigma has a direct impact on your ability to heal, because healing requires connection, and stigma blocks connection.

In a conventional affair, the betrayed woman has access to a well-established support infrastructure. Friends understand. Family understands. Therapists have frameworks. Support groups exist. The cultural script, while painful, is at least familiar: he cheated, she's heartbroken, she needs support. But when the affair involves a trans woman or femboy, the script breaks. The support infrastructure falters. The people you would normally turn to don't know how to respond because they don't understand the situation, and their confusion compounds your isolation.

The stigma operates on multiple levels simultaneously. There is the heteronormative level: the assumption that your man's involvement with a trans woman means he's gay, which carries its own set of social judgments. There is the transphobic level: the cultural disgust toward transgender people that gets projected onto you by association, as if his attraction somehow contaminates you. There is the racial level: in Black communities specifically, the DL narrative carries decades of fear, shame, and moral panic that get activated the moment this topic surfaces. And there is the gendered level: the expectation that a "good woman" should have been able to keep her man satisfied, and the implication that you failed at your womanly duty.

Every single one of these stigmas is a lie. They are cultural constructions that serve no purpose other than to make you feel worse about a situation that is already devastating. And the work of deprogramming shame is the work of identifying these lies, naming them, and refusing to carry them.

Paulette's Story

Paulette is forty-six and lives in Baltimore. She is a deaconess at her church. When she discovered her husband's involvement with a trans woman, her first fear wasn't about her marriage. It was about her church.

"I knew that if this got out, I wouldn't just lose my husband," Paulette said. "I would lose my standing. My position. My community. People who had looked up to me for twenty years would look at me differently. Not with sympathy, with something worse. A combination of pity and disgust that I wouldn't be able to survive. So I said nothing. For eighteen months, I carried the weight of it alone, pretending everything was fine at church on Sunday morning while my entire world was falling apart."

Paulette eventually confided in one person: a retired pastor from a neighboring church who was known for his compassion and confidentiality. "He didn't flinch," she said. "He didn't judge. He said, 'Sister Paulette, this is not your sin to carry. You didn't do this. Let me help you set it down.' Those words saved my life. Because the shame was literally killing me. My blood pressure was out of control. I was having chest pains. My doctor told me I was on the path to a heart attack. The shame was living in my body, and it was destroying me from the inside out."

When Shame Lives in the Body: The Physical Cost of Carrying It

Paulette's experience is not unusual. Shame is not just an emotion, it's a physiological state. When you are carrying shame, your body responds as if it is under constant threat. Cortisol, the stress hormone, remains elevated. Your blood pressure rises. Your immune system weakens. Your sleep is disrupted. Your appetite is suppressed or, in some cases, becomes uncontrollable in the other direction. Your body tenses in ways you don't even notice: jaw clenching, shoulder tightening, stomach knotting. Over weeks and months, these physical responses compound into real health problems.

I mention this not to frighten you but to validate you. If you have been experiencing physical symptoms since the discovery, headaches, stomach problems, chest tightness, unexplained pain, dramatic weight changes, hair loss, skin problems, you are not imagining it. Your body is responding to the emotional burden you are carrying. And one of the most important steps in the healing process is recognizing that the shame you're carrying is making you physically sick and deciding that your health matters more than his secret.

Taking care of your body during this time is not selfish. It is essential. See your doctor. Get a full checkup. Be honest about what you're going through, your physician can't help you if they don't know the full picture. Address the sleep issues, the appetite issues, the stress response. Your body has been in crisis mode, and it needs active intervention to come down from that state. You cannot heal your heart if your body is breaking down around it.

Practical Tools: Exercises for Deprogramming Shame

Therapy is the most powerful tool for processing shame, and I cannot recommend it strongly enough. But there are also practices you can incorporate into your daily life that support the deprogramming process. These are not substitutes for professional help. They are companions to it.

The Separation Exercise

Every time a shame thought arises, "I wasn't enough," "I should have known," "Something is wrong with me", practice separating the thought from the truth. Say to yourself, either silently or out loud: "That is his story, not mine. His choices are about him. My worth is not determined by his decisions." The first hundred times you say it, you won't believe it. That's normal. Keep saying it. Neurological research on cognitive reframing shows that repeated practice of alternative narratives gradually weakens the neural pathways that maintain shame-based beliefs. You are literally rewiring your brain, one repetition at a time.

The Witness Exercise

Write down your story as if you were telling it about someone else. Not "I found out my husband was seeing a trans woman" but "She found out her husband was seeing a trans woman." Read it back. Notice how much more compassion you feel for that third-person woman than you feel for yourself. That compassion is the correct response. Now redirect it inward. You deserve the same compassion you would give a stranger in your situation. The shame you carry is preventing you from giving yourself what you would freely give anyone else.

The Inventory Exercise

Make a list of everything you are, not in relation to him, but independently. Your skills, your qualities, your accomplishments, your relationships, your values, your contributions to the world. This is not vanity. This is a corrective to the distortion that betrayal creates. Betrayal makes you feel like your entire identity has been reduced to one thing: the woman whose man was involved with a trans woman. But you are a thousand things besides that. You were a thousand things before him, and you will be a thousand things after this crisis passes. The inventory is a reminder of the fullness of who you are: a fullness that his choices cannot diminish.

The Time Horizon Exercise

When the shame feels suffocating, project yourself forward in time. Ask yourself: "Will I still feel this same intensity of shame in five years?" The answer, based on every woman I've spoken with who is further along in the process, is no. The acute shame passes. It does not disappear overnight, but it diminishes, steadily, measurably, as you do the work of separating his choices from your identity. The women who are five and ten years out from this discovery describe the shame as a memory, not a current state. A scar, not a wound. You will get there. The path is painful, but the destination is real.

Building Your Support Network When You Feel You Can't Tell Anyone

The isolation that comes with this type of discovery is one of its most damaging aspects. You need support, but you feel you can't access it. So how do you build a support network when the nature of your situation makes you feel like you can't tell anyone?

Start with one person. Not the person who will have the biggest reaction. Not the person who will tell everyone else. Choose the person in your life who has demonstrated the most consistent capacity for empathy, discretion, and non-judgment. The friend who sat with you during a crisis without trying to fix it. The family member who listens more than they advise. The colleague who has shared their own vulnerability with you in a way that told you they could handle yours. Start there. Tell that one person as much or as little as you need to. The relief of having even one person who knows your truth can be transformative.

Find a therapist who specializes in both infidelity and LGBTQ issues. This is not optional: it is essential. A therapist who is experienced with infidelity but not LGBTQ-affirming may inadvertently reinforce the stigma by treating the gender identity element as the central problem. A therapist who is LGBTQ-affirming but not experienced with infidelity may underestimate the betrayal trauma. You need someone who can hold both dimensions simultaneously. Ask directly during your initial consultation: "Do you have experience working with women whose partners have been involved with transgender individuals?" If the answer is no, keep looking.

Consider online support communities. Organizations and forums exist for partners of individuals dealing with complex sexuality issues. While I won't name specific forums, because they change and evolve, a focused online search for "support for wives of DL men" or "partner support for mixed-orientation relationships" will lead you to spaces where other women have navigated exactly what you're going through. Reading their stories, even if you never post your own, can break the isolation that makes you feel like you're the only woman in the world dealing with this.

And draw on your faith, if you have one; but be strategic about where. If your church is a place of genuine compassion and confidentiality, your pastor or a trusted church counselor may be a resource. But if your church is a place where this type of revelation would be met with gossip, judgment, or theological condemnation, protect yourself. Your spiritual life can sustain you through this crisis, but the institutional church may not be the safest vessel for it right now. Pray in private. Read in private. Connect with God or your higher power in whatever way feeds your soul without exposing your wound to people who might pour salt into it.

I also want to say something specifically to my sisters in the Black community, because I know how our networks operate and I know the particular risks you face. In our community, information moves fast and judgment moves faster. The church mothers talk. The group chat talks. The beauty shop talks. And the fear of being the subject of that talk can keep you locked in silence for years. But your silence is not protecting you: it is imprisoning you. And the women in your life who are worth keeping will respond to your truth with love, not with gossip. If you don't know who those women are, this crisis will reveal them. The ones who stay, who hold you, who don't flinch, those are your people. The ones who whisper, who distance, who use your pain for entertainment, those were never your people. Better to know now.

Your support network doesn't have to be large. It just has to be real. One good therapist. One trustworthy friend. One space, online or in person, where you can speak your truth without editing it for someone else's comfort. That's enough to start. That's enough to break the isolation. And breaking the isolation is how you begin to break the shame.

Beginning the Journey: From Shame to Self-Worth

Deprogramming shame is not a single event. It's a process: a daily discipline of catching the shame narrative when it starts, interrupting it, and replacing it with truth. Here are the truths I want you to carry forward from this chapter:

You are not inadequate. His attraction is about the breadth of his desire, not the insufficiency of yours.

You could not have prevented this. His choices were his own, and the infrastructure of deception he built was specifically designed to keep you from knowing.

Your relationship was real. The love, the intimacy, the years you shared, none of it was fake. It was real and it was also incomplete, because he was hiding a part of himself. Both things are true.

You are not alone. Other women have stood exactly where you're standing, felt exactly what you're feeling, and found their way through. You will too.

What happened to you is not your shame to carry. It is his. He made the choices. He built the lies. He created the situation. Your only job now is to take care of yourself, to heal, to process, to grieve, and eventually, to reclaim the sense of self-worth that the discovery tried to steal from you.

Denitra's Words

I'll close this chapter with something Denitra, a forty-seven-year-old woman from Cleveland, said to me three years after she discovered her husband's involvement with a trans woman. She had been through therapy, through grief, through rage, through the worst of it. She was sitting across from me at a coffee shop, looking more at peace than anyone in her situation has a right to look. I asked her what got her through.

"One day," she said, "I looked in the mirror and I said out loud: 'This is not about me.' And I meant it. Not in my head, in my gut. In my bones. I had been carrying his secret like it was my failure for over a year. And that morning, I just… set it down. I looked at myself and I saw a woman who had been lied to. Not a woman who was lacking. A woman who was lied to. And there is a world of difference between those two things."

Denitra paused, then smiled. "I still have hard days. I still get angry. I still sometimes wonder. But the shame? The shame is gone. Because I finally understood: it was never mine to carry in the first place."

That is the destination this chapter is pointing you toward. Not the absence of pain, pain is part of the process. But the absence of shame. The ability to separate what was done to you from who you are. The knowledge that your womanhood is whole, your femininity is complete, and the fracture in your life was caused by someone else's choices, not by anything you lacked.

I want to speak to you directly for a moment, not as an author but as someone who has watched this story unfold in real people's lives, in real time, for years. I have seen women at the bottom of this. I have seen them in the fetal position on their bathroom floor at two in the morning, convinced they were worthless. I have seen the same women, two years later, standing upright, eyes clear, voice steady, living lives that are fuller and more authentic than anything they had before the discovery. The journey between those two versions of the same woman is the hardest thing most of them have ever done. But every single one of them told me the same thing: it was worth it. Not because the pain was worth it: the pain was terrible. But because the person they became on the other side of the pain was someone they actually liked. Someone who knew her own value. Someone who would never again let another person's choices determine her sense of self.

You will be that woman. Not today. Maybe not tomorrow. But you are already on the path, because you are here, reading, refusing to let the shame have the last word. And that refusal, that stubborn, courageous insistence on clarity and self-worth, is the beginning of everything.

The next chapter turns to a practical and critical topic: your physical health. Because the betrayal didn't just affect your heart and your mind. It may have affected your body too. And protecting your body is an act of self-love that you deserve, right now, today, without waiting another minute.

CHAPTER NINE

The Health Conversation: Protecting Yourself Physically

This chapter might be the most difficult one to read, and it is without question the most important one to act on. Because while the emotional dimensions of this situation will take months or years to process, the health dimensions require immediate attention. Today. Not after the conversation. Not after therapy. Not after you've decided what to do about the relationship. Now.

I'm going to give you the medical information you need in plain language, without euphemism, and without judgment toward anyone. This chapter is not about stigmatizing trans women, femboys, or anyone in the LGBTQIA community. It is about the simple, clinical reality that your partner has been having sexual contact outside of your relationship without your knowledge or consent. That means you have been exposed to risk without being given the opportunity to protect yourself. And that is a violation of your bodily autonomy that requires an immediate medical response.

I want to be clear about the framing: the health risk in your situation comes from having a partner with concurrent sexual partnerships, which is a risk factor regardless of the gender identity of the other person involved. A man who secretly has sex with a cisgender woman also puts his wife at risk. The risk here is about secrecy and concurrent partnerships, not about the trans community.

Understanding the Risk: Why Concurrent Partnerships Are Dangerous

Public health research has long established that concurrent sexual partnerships, where an individual maintains sexual relationships with multiple people during overlapping time periods, represent a significantly higher risk for STI transmission than sequential partnerships. The reason is mathematical: in a network of concurrent partnerships, an infection acquired by any one person can rapidly spread to all other members of the network, because the connections are active simultaneously.

Here is what that means for you specifically. Your partner was having sex with you and with at least one other person during the same time period. That other person may have also had other sexual partners. Each person in that chain represents a potential point of entry for infection. And because these partnerships were secret, nobody in the chain had complete information about their actual risk. You didn't know about her. She may or may not have known about you. And he may not have known about any other partners his other partner may have had. The secrecy doesn't just violate trust: it destroys the ability of everyone in the network to make informed decisions about their own health.

I am not saying that your partner's other partner was necessarily promiscuous or unhealthy. Trans women, like all people, range from completely monogamous to sexually active with multiple partners. The point is that you don't know; and your partner, regardless of what he claims, may not know either. In the absence of complete information, comprehensive testing is the only responsible course of action.

The Truth About Condom Use in DL Relationships

One of the first questions women ask after discovery is: "Did he use protection?" The honest answer, based on the conversations I've had with DL men and their partners, is: sometimes. And sometimes is not enough when it comes to your health.

Research on men who have sex with transgender women has consistently found that condom use in these relationships is inconsistent. The reasons are complex. In the early stages of a DL relationship, particularly when the encounters are casual or transactional, condom use tends to be more consistent. But as the relationship deepens, as emotional intimacy develops, as the encounter shifts from a transaction to a partnership, condom use often decreases or stops altogether. The man begins to trust his partner. The partner begins to trust him. And condoms, which represent a barrier, a reminder that this is not a "real" relationship, get discarded because they feel incompatible with the emotional connection both parties have developed.

This means that the longer your partner's secret relationship lasted, the less likely it is that protection was used consistently. A man who had a one-time encounter may have used a condom. A man who maintained a two-year emotional relationship almost certainly did not use one every time. And a single unprotected encounter is all it takes.

Your partner may tell you that he "always used protection." He may even believe it, memory is flexible, and guilt has a way of editing the past. But his word is not a substitute for your test results. Trust the results.

What You Need to Get Tested For: A Complete List

If you have learned or suspect that your partner has been sexually active outside your relationship, you need comprehensive STI screening. Not a partial screening. Not just the tests your doctor typically runs at an annual checkup. A comprehensive panel. Here is what that includes:

HIV

This is the one most women fear, and the one you need to address first. Modern HIV testing is fast, accurate, and available at most clinics, pharmacies, and health departments. The standard screening is a combination antigen/antibody test, which can detect HIV as early as eighteen to forty-five days after exposure. If you believe the exposure may have been recent, within the last seventy-two hours, ask your doctor about post-exposure prophylaxis, or PEP, which is a course of antiretroviral medication that can significantly reduce the risk of HIV infection if started promptly. If the exposure is ongoing and you are not yet ready to stop having sex with your partner, ask your doctor about pre-exposure prophylaxis, or PrEP, which is a daily medication that provides substantial protection against HIV when taken consistently.

Syphilis

Syphilis has been surging in the United States. The CDC reported nearly four thousand cases of congenital syphilis in 2024 alone: a staggering increase from a decade ago. Syphilis is transmitted through direct contact with a syphilis sore, which can occur during vaginal, anal, or oral sex. Testing involves a simple blood draw. Syphilis is curable with antibiotics when caught early, but untreated syphilis can cause serious long-term health complications including damage to the heart, brain, and nervous system.

Chlamydia and Gonorrhea

These are the two most commonly reported bacterial STIs in the United States, with over two million combined cases reported to the CDC in 2024. Both can be asymptomatic, meaning you can have them without knowing it, and both can cause serious complications if left untreated, including pelvic inflammatory disease, chronic pelvic pain, and infertility. Testing typically involves a urine sample or a swab, and both are curable with antibiotics. If your partner has had oral or anal sexual contact outside the relationship, request extragenital testing as well, throat and rectal swabs, since infections at these sites are often asymptomatic and are missed by standard urogenital testing alone.

Hepatitis B and C

Hepatitis B is transmitted through sexual contact, and hepatitis C, while less commonly sexually transmitted, can be transmitted during sexual activity that involves blood-to-blood contact. Both can be asymptomatic for years while causing progressive liver damage. Blood tests for both are straightforward. If you have not been vaccinated for hepatitis B, this is an appropriate time to discuss vaccination with your healthcare provider.

Herpes (HSV-1 and HSV-2)

Herpes is extremely common: the CDC estimates that approximately one in eight Americans between ages fourteen and forty-nine has genital HSV-2 infection, though some sources still cite the older estimate of one in six. It can be transmitted even when no symptoms are present. Testing for herpes is usually done through a blood test that detects antibodies, though the CDC does not recommend routine herpes screening for people without symptoms. However, given your specific situation, where your partner has had undisclosed sexual contact, requesting a herpes test is reasonable and appropriate.

HPV

Human papillomavirus is the most common STI in the United States. While most HPV infections clear on their own, certain strains can cause genital warts and cervical cancer. If you are due for a Pap smear or HPV test, schedule one. If you are under forty-five and have not completed the HPV vaccine series, discuss vaccination with your provider.

Trichomoniasis

Trichomoniasis is caused by a parasite and is the most common curable STI. It can be asymptomatic in many people and is often missed because it is not included in standard STI panels unless specifically requested. Ask for a trichomoniasis test. Treatment is a simple course of oral antibiotics.

Mpox

Mpox, formerly known as monkeypox, is primarily spread through close physical contact. While the major outbreaks of recent years primarily affected men who have sex with men, the virus can be transmitted through any close physical contact. If your partner has had sexual contact outside your relationship, particularly with partners in networks where mpox has circulated, mention this to your healthcare provider.

How to Get Tested: Practical Steps

You have several options for comprehensive STI testing, and the right one depends on your circumstances, your insurance, and your comfort level.

Your primary care physician is the most straightforward option. Schedule an appointment and tell your doctor that you need a full STI screening. You do not have to explain why. You do not have to disclose the details of your situation. Simply saying "I need a comprehensive STI panel" is sufficient. A good doctor will not interrogate you.

Planned Parenthood and similar reproductive health clinics offer comprehensive STI testing, often on a sliding scale based on income. Many locations offer walk-in testing without an appointment. These clinics are experienced in providing testing in a non-judgmental, confidential environment.

Your local health department likely offers free or low-cost STI testing. Hours and availability vary, but this is an option for women who are uninsured or who want to avoid using their regular healthcare provider for privacy reasons.

At-home STI testing kits are available from several companies and can be ordered online. These kits allow you to collect samples at home and mail them to a lab for analysis. Results are typically available within a few days. While these kits are convenient, they may not test for every infection, so verify the panel before ordering. At-home kits are particularly useful for women who live in small communities where walking into the local clinic might raise questions, or for women who are not yet ready to discuss their situation with anyone face-to-face.

Regardless of which testing option you choose, here are a few practical tips. First, request a copy of your results for your own records, do not rely on the clinic or your doctor's office to keep your records accessible. Second, if your insurance is shared with your partner and you don't want him to see the claim, many clinics and health departments offer confidential or anonymous testing that does not bill insurance. Third, if the idea of going alone feels overwhelming, bring your one trusted person: the friend or family member you identified in the previous chapter. You don't have to do this alone. Having someone in the waiting room, even if they don't go back with you, can make the difference between making it through the appointment and falling apart.

I also want to acknowledge something that women in this situation have told me over and over: the waiting is the worst part. The days between the blood draw and the results call can feel like an eternity. Your mind will run through every worst-case scenario. You will convince yourself that something is wrong, that the doctor is delaying the call because the news is bad, that your life is about to change forever. This anxiety is normal. It does not mean something is wrong. It means you are under extraordinary stress and your brain is doing what brains do under stress, catastrophizing. Breathe. Distract yourself if you can. And remind yourself that regardless of what the results say, you have already done the hardest part: you showed up. You took action. You chose yourself.

Tanya's Story

Tanya is thirty-seven and lives in Atlanta. When she discovered her husband Marcus's three-year relationship with a trans woman, her first call, before she confronted him, before she called her sister, before she called a lawyer, was to her gynecologist.

"I was terrified," Tanya told me. "Not just of what I might find out, but of having to explain why I needed the tests. I couldn't bring myself to tell my doctor what had happened. So I just said, 'I need a full panel. Everything.' She didn't ask why. She just ordered the tests. And that act, picking up the phone, making the appointment, driving to the office, sitting in that chair, was the first thing I did for myself after the discovery. It was the first time I stopped spinning and took an action that was purely about protecting me."

Tanya's results came back clear. She was lucky. But she told me that even if the results had been different, she was glad she went. "Knowing is always better than not knowing. The uncertainty was eating me alive. At least when the results came back, I could take one fear off the table and focus on the others."

If Your Results Come Back Positive: What to Know

I need to prepare you for the possibility that your test results may not all be negative. If that happens, here is what I want you to know:

Most common STIs are curable. Chlamydia, gonorrhea, syphilis, and trichomoniasis are all treated and cured with antibiotics. A positive result for any of these is not a life sentence. It is a treatable medical condition that requires a course of medication and follow-up testing to confirm clearance. Your doctor will walk you through the treatment plan, which in most cases is straightforward and brief.

Herpes and HPV are manageable. While neither has a cure, both are extremely common and manageable with appropriate medical care. Herpes can be managed with antiviral medications that reduce outbreak frequency and transmission risk. Most HPV infections clear on their own within two years, and the strains that don't can be monitored through regular screening to catch any cellular changes early.

An HIV-positive result is not the end. Modern antiretroviral therapy has transformed HIV from a death sentence into a manageable chronic condition. People living with HIV who take their medication consistently can achieve an undetectable viral load, which means they cannot transmit the virus to sexual partners. If you receive an HIV-positive result, you will be connected with an infectious disease specialist who will develop a treatment plan. This is devastating news, and you will need support processing it; but you will survive it, and you will live a full life.

A positive result is not your fault. I cannot say this strongly enough. If you test positive for any STI, the infection was transmitted to you by someone who did not give you the information you needed to protect yourself. You are not dirty. You are not damaged. You are a person who was exposed to an infection through no fault of your own. The stigma surrounding STIs is powerful, and it may compound the shame you are already carrying from the betrayal. Reject that stigma. You did nothing wrong. You got tested, which is the responsible thing to do. And now you are getting treated, which is the right thing to do.

Janelle's Story

Janelle is thirty-five and lives in Chicago. Her test results came back positive for both chlamydia and HSV-2. She told me that receiving those results felt like being betrayed all over again.

"The chlamydia, they told me, was treatable. One round of antibiotics and it would be gone. And it was. But the herpes, that's forever. That's something I carry in my body for the rest of my life because of a choice he made. He didn't just break my heart. He changed my body. Permanently. And I had no say in it."

Janelle went through a period of intense grief after the diagnosis, grief for her health, grief for her sense of bodily integrity, grief for the future relationships that she feared would be complicated by her HSV-2 status. But she also found, through therapy and through connecting with other women living with herpes, that the stigma was far worse than the reality.

"Millions of people have herpes," Janelle told me. "Millions. My doctor told me that about one in eight adults has HSV-2. I'm not a freak. I'm not damaged goods. I'm a woman who got an extremely common infection from a man who lied to me. And I refuse, I absolutely refuse, to let his lie define my body or my future. I take my medication. I manage it. And I have moved on with my life. The herpes is a footnote, not a headline."

Having the Health Conversation with Your Partner

At some point, you will need to have a conversation with your partner about sexual health. This conversation may happen as part of the larger confrontation about his secret life, or it may happen separately. Either way, it is essential; because your health going forward depends on having accurate information about his sexual history and his current STI status.

If you have not yet confronted him about what you know, you can request STI testing without revealing the reason. You can frame it as a routine health decision: "My doctor recommended that we both get tested as part of our annual checkup." You can frame it as something you saw in the news: "I was reading about the rise in syphilis cases and I think we should both get screened." You can frame it in any way that gets him to a clinic without triggering a confrontation you're not yet ready for.

If you have already confronted him, the conversation is more direct. You need to know: who he has been sexually active with, what kind of sexual contact occurred, whether protection was used consistently, and whether he has been tested recently. His answers may not be fully honest, given that his entire secret life was built on dishonesty, you should approach his answers with appropriate skepticism and rely on your own test results rather than his assurances.

Regardless of what he says, get tested yourself. Do not rely on his word that he was "always safe" or that his other partner was "clean." In the context of DL behavior, where secrecy and deception are the defining features, his assurances about sexual health carry zero weight. Your test results are the only information you can trust.

Protecting Yourself Going Forward

Whether you stay in the relationship or leave, you need to make informed decisions about your ongoing sexual health. If you choose to remain in the relationship while you process and decide, consider the following:

Condom use is non-negotiable. Until you have clarity about the full scope of his sexual activity and until both of you have been tested and received results, insisting on condom use with your partner is not an insult: it is a basic health precaution. If he resists, that resistance itself tells you something about his regard for your safety.

Consider PrEP. Pre-exposure prophylaxis is a daily medication that significantly reduces the risk of HIV infection. It is available by prescription and is covered by most insurance plans. If there is any possibility that your partner is continuing sexual activity outside the relationship, PrEP provides an additional layer of protection that you control.

Schedule follow-up testing. Some STIs, particularly HIV and syphilis, can have window periods, meaning they may not show up on tests immediately after exposure. Your initial test may come back clear, but follow-up testing at three months and six months is recommended to ensure nothing was missed during the window period. Mark these dates in your calendar now. Set reminders on your phone. Treat them as non-negotiable medical appointments, because they are.

Monitor your own body. Pay attention to any unusual symptoms: discharge, itching, sores, pain during urination, pelvic pain, unusual bleeding. Many STIs are asymptomatic, but if symptoms do appear, seek medical attention immediately. Do not dismiss symptoms or attribute them to stress. Your body is communicating, listen to it.

Talk to your doctor about vaccination. In addition to the HPV vaccine mentioned earlier, ensure your hepatitis B vaccination is up to date. Vaccines are one of the few tools you have to proactively prevent infection, and using every available tool is wise in this situation.

Document everything. Keep records of your test dates, results, and any treatments received. If your situation leads to legal proceedings, divorce, custody disputes, or in some jurisdictions, criminal charges related to knowing STI transmission, your medical records may be relevant. Store this documentation securely.

Patricia's Lesson

Patricia, whom we met in Chapter 5, shared a health dimension to her story that she wanted other women to know about. After discovering her husband Gregory's four-year relationship with a trans woman named Diamond, Patricia got tested. Her results revealed that she had contracted chlamydia: an infection she had no symptoms of and would not have discovered without testing.

"I felt violated all over again," Patricia said. "The emotional betrayal was one thing. But learning that he had put my physical health at risk, that his choices had literally entered my body without my knowledge or consent, that was a different kind of violation. It felt criminal. Because in a very real sense, it was. I didn't consent to being exposed to anything. He made that decision for me."

Patricia was treated successfully and has had no complications. But she said the experience changed her perspective on the entire situation. "Up until that point, part of me was still trying to minimize what he'd done. Still trying to make it manageable. But the chlamydia diagnosis made it real in a way that the emotional stuff, as painful as it was, hadn't. He had endangered my health. He had endangered my fertility, I was forty-seven, past childbearing, but the principle was the same. If I had been younger, an untreated infection could have cost me the ability to have children. That's not just a betrayal. That's reckless endangerment."

Finding a Healthcare Provider Who Understands

Not all healthcare providers are equally equipped to handle the complexity of your situation. When seeking STI testing and ongoing sexual health care in the context of a DL relationship, look for a provider who demonstrates the following qualities:

Non-judgmental communication. Your provider should not react with shock, moral judgment, or visible discomfort when you describe your situation. If they do, find a different provider. You are dealing with enough judgment from the world. Your doctor's office should be a judgment-free zone.

Comprehensive testing practices. A good provider will order a full panel without having to be asked twice and will include extragenital testing when appropriate. If your provider tries to minimize the need for testing or says "you probably don't need all that," advocate for yourself. You know what you've been exposed to. You have the right to a thorough evaluation.

Familiarity with LGBTQ health issues. A provider who understands the health dynamics relevant to LGBTQ populations will be better equipped to assess your risk profile and recommend appropriate testing and preventive measures. Federally Qualified Health Centers, university-affiliated clinics, and Planned Parenthood locations tend to have strong LGBTQ-inclusive practices.

Willingness to discuss PrEP. If your provider is unfamiliar with PrEP or dismisses it as "not for women," that provider is not up to date on current clinical guidelines. PrEP is approved for anyone at risk of HIV, and a woman whose partner has undisclosed concurrent sexual partnerships meets that criterion.

Gail's Story

Gail is fifty-three and lives in Philadelphia. She is a retired school administrator, and she approached her health situation with the same systematic thoroughness that she brought to her career. When she discovered her husband Vernon's involvement with a trans woman, she made a list of every clinic in the city that offered comprehensive STI testing, called three of them, and chose the one that could see her fastest.

"I didn't even tell Vernon I was going," Gail said. "I wasn't ready to have the conversation yet. But I was ready to take care of myself. I walked into that clinic and told the nurse, 'I need everything. HIV, syphilis, chlamydia, gonorrhea, hepatitis, herpes, trich. Everything you have, I want it.' The nurse didn't blink. She said, 'We can do all of that.' And forty-five minutes later, I had been tested for everything."

Gail's results came back positive for HPV: a strain that required monitoring but not immediate treatment. "It could have been worse," she said. "And it made me angry, because this was a man who stood before God and promised to forsake all others. He didn't just break a vow. He compromised my body. But I'll tell you something: getting tested was the single most empowering thing I did in that entire first month. Everything else felt like it was happening to me. The testing was something I chose. I chose to protect myself. And that choice gave me back a piece of the control his lies had taken."

A Sensitive Note: If You Are Pregnant or Trying to Conceive

If you are currently pregnant or were recently pregnant during the period when your partner was sexually active outside the relationship, please tell your obstetrician about the situation as soon as possible. Certain STIs, particularly syphilis, chlamydia, and gonorrhea, can be transmitted to a baby during pregnancy or delivery, with serious consequences including premature birth, low birth weight, eye infections, pneumonia, and in the case of congenital syphilis, stillbirth or severe developmental complications.

Congenital syphilis in particular has reached crisis levels in the United States, with cases increasing dramatically year over year. If you were pregnant while your partner had undisclosed sexual partners, your prenatal syphilis screening results should be reviewed, and additional testing may be warranted. This is not optional: it is a matter of your baby's safety.

If you are trying to conceive, postpone attempts until both you and your partner have been fully tested and received clear results. The window periods for certain infections mean that a single negative test may not be sufficient, follow-up testing at three and six months provides more complete assurance. I know this is painful to hear when family planning is already an emotional topic. But bringing a healthy child into the world requires knowing that both parents are healthy. Your future child deserves that certainty.

The Intersection of Physical and Emotional Health

Your physical health and your emotional health are not separate systems. They are deeply interconnected, and the stress of this situation is affecting both simultaneously. The betrayal trauma we discussed in the previous chapter produces physical symptoms, elevated cortisol, disrupted sleep, suppressed immune function, that can make you more vulnerable to infection and slower to recover from illness. Taking care of your physical health is therefore not separate from taking care of your emotional health. It is the same project.

The Legal Dimension: What You Should Know

I am not a lawyer, and this section is not legal advice. But you should be aware that in many states, knowingly exposing a partner to an STI without disclosure is a crime. The laws vary significantly by jurisdiction, some states criminalize knowing transmission of specific infections like HIV, while others have broader statutes covering reckless endangerment or fraud. If you have contracted an STI from your partner and he knew about, or should have known about, his risk status, you may have legal options.

Consult with a family law attorney, particularly if you are considering divorce. In many jurisdictions, a partner's infidelity and it's health consequences can be relevant to divorce proceedings, spousal support determinations, and custody arrangements. Some women have successfully pursued civil claims for damages related to STI transmission. Whether or not you pursue legal action, knowing your options gives you information, and information gives you power.

Even if you choose not to pursue legal action, your medical documentation may be important in other contexts. If the situation leads to divorce, having documented evidence that you sought medical care as a result of his behavior strengthens your position. If you need to explain health-related absences to an employer, having records provides cover. If you apply for life insurance or face medical underwriting in the future, having a clear timeline of when and how you were exposed protects you from being penalized for his choices.

A Word About His Health

This may feel counterintuitive given everything you are going through, but I want to mention it briefly: your partner needs to get tested too. Regardless of the state of your relationship, regardless of your feelings toward him, his health status affects your health status as long as you are in any kind of sexual contact. If he has not been tested; and many DL men have not, precisely because testing would make the secret life feel more real: he needs to be.

Some women choose to require testing as a condition of continuing any conversation about the relationship. "We don't talk about us until we both have results" is a perfectly reasonable boundary. It establishes that your health is a non-negotiable priority and that the days of him making unilateral decisions about your shared health are over.

If he refuses to get tested, that refusal tells you everything you need to know about his willingness to take responsibility for the consequences of his actions. A man who will not even get a blood draw to protect the health of the woman he claims to love is a man who is still prioritizing his comfort over your safety. And that pattern, his comfort over your safety, is the exact pattern that created this entire situation.

Make your health appointments. Get the tests. Follow up on the results. Take the medications if they are prescribed. And while you are at the doctor's office, mention the stress you are under. Ask about sleep support if you need it. Ask about anxiety management. Ask about referrals to a therapist if you don't already have one. Your doctor can be a gateway to the broader support system you need right now.

I want to address one more thing before we close this chapter: the anger. Many women tell me that the health dimension is the one that transforms their grief into rage. They can process the emotional betrayal. They can even, with time, process the gender identity dimension. But the realization that their partner risked their physical health: that he exposed them to potential infection, potential infertility, potential life-altering illness, without their knowledge or consent, is the betrayal that feels unforgivable. And I understand that anger. It is justified. Your body is your most fundamental possession. And he treated it with a recklessness that no amount of love or remorse can fully excuse.

Channel that anger into action. Let the anger be the fuel that drives you to the clinic. Let it be the energy that makes you pick up the phone and schedule the appointment you've been putting off. Let it be the force that makes you insist on condoms, demand transparency, and refuse to accept "I was always safe" as a substitute for test results. Anger, when directed properly, is one of the most powerful tools you have. Use it.

I'll say it one more time: get tested. Today. Not next week. Today. If the clinic is closed today, make the appointment first thing tomorrow morning. This is the single most concrete, actionable step you can take to protect yourself, and it is entirely within your control. You cannot control his behavior. You cannot control the past. But you can walk into a clinic, get a comprehensive screening, and know, with certainty, where your health stands. That knowledge is power. That knowledge is freedom. And that knowledge is an act of self-love that you owe to yourself.

The next chapter shifts the perspective entirely. We're going to hear directly from the other sides of this dynamic, trans women, femboys, and DL men speaking in their own voices about their experiences, their motivations, and what they want the women in their lives to understand. It is the most unusual chapter in the book, and possibly the most illuminating.

CHAPTER TEN

Conversations with the Other Side: Voices from Trans Women, Femboys, and DL Men

Up to this point, this book has been written primarily for you: the woman. Your perspective, your pain, your decisions have been at the center of every chapter. That was intentional, because you are the person this book was designed to serve. But understanding your situation fully requires hearing from the other people inside it. This chapter gives them the floor.

What follows are composite voices drawn from extensive conversations with trans women who have dated DL men, femboys who have been in secret relationships with men who presented as straight, and DL men who were willing to speak honestly about their experiences. These voices are not here to make you sympathize with anyone. They are not here to excuse behavior. They are here because every person I interviewed for this book asked me the same question: "Will you let me say what I need to say to her?" Her being you. The woman who never knew they existed.

I said yes. And I think, if you can read this chapter with an open heart, you will find that it gives you something no other chapter can: the complete picture. Not just your piece of it. All of it.

The Trans Women Speak

Serena: "I Am Not Your Enemy"

Serena is thirty-four and lives in a mid-sized city in the South. She has been involved with three DL men over the past decade. Two were married. One had a long-term girlfriend. All of them came to her. All of them pursued her. And all of them, eventually, disappeared back into their public lives when the risk of discovery became too real.

"The first thing I want the wives and girlfriends to know is that I didn't set out to take your man. I know that's hard to believe, but it's true. I was on an app, living my life, and he found me. He messaged me. He pursued me. He told me he was single, or separated, or 'in the process of leaving.' By the time I found out the truth, I was already in deep. And by then, the feelings were real."

"The second thing I want you to know is that being the secret is not glamorous. It's not exciting. It's lonely. You get the scraps: a few hours on a Tuesday afternoon, a text at midnight when he's sure you're asleep, a gift he bought with cash so it wouldn't show up on a statement. You don't get the holidays. You don't get the family dinners. You don't get introduced to his friends. You exist in a bubble, and that bubble is the only space in his life where you're allowed to be real."

"And the third thing, the thing I most want to say, is this: I am not your enemy. I know it feels that way. I know looking at a picture of me probably makes your stomach turn. But I was lied to, too. He lied to both of us. He used both of us. And the pain I carry from being someone's secret for years is not so different from the pain you carry from being someone's fool. Different shape, same source. And that source is him."

Diamond: "The Holidays Were the Worst"

Diamond is forty-two and lives in Norfolk, Virginia. She was involved with a married man named Gregory for four years. We met Gregory's wife Patricia in Chapter 5.

"Every Thanksgiving, every Christmas, every New Year's Eve, I sat in my apartment alone while he was at home carving the turkey with his family. He'd text me 'Merry Christmas, beautiful' at midnight, after everyone was asleep. And I'd be lying in my bed, staring at that message, thinking: This is my life. This is what I accepted. A midnight text while his wife got the whole man."

"I want his wife to know something: I didn't hate her. I envied her. She had the thing I wanted most, not Gregory specifically, but the life. The house. The dinner table. The public love. She had a man who claimed her. I had a man who hid me. And every time he left my apartment to drive home to her, a part of me wondered: Why am I not enough to be claimed? And then I'd realize, it's not about being enough. It's about a man who built a system where he could have both without ever having to choose. He didn't choose her over me. He didn't choose me over her. He chose himself over both of us."

Valentina: "We Talk About Your Husbands"

Valentina is twenty-eight and lives in New York City. She is active in the trans community and has a large social media following. She has not been in a long-term relationship with a DL man, but she has been pursued by dozens of them; and she has watched her friends navigate these dynamics for years.

"The wives think this is hidden. It's not. Not on our side. We know who your husbands are. We know their real names, where they work, what church they go to. We show each other the DMs. We compare notes. Not to be cruel, to be safe. Because some of these men are dangerous when they feel exposed. Some of them have threatened trans women who tried to go public. Some have been violent. So we share information the way you'd share information about a bad neighborhood: to protect each other."

"But here's what I want the wives to understand: we're not laughing at you. We're not celebrating that your man is in our DMs. Most of us find it sad. Because we know the pain that's coming for you, and we know there's nothing we can do to prevent it. Some of my friends have actually warned the wives, sent anonymous messages, dropped hints. It almost never ends well. The wife doesn't want to hear it from us. I get it. But the information is there if she ever wants it."

Carmen: "I Stopped Dating DL Men"

Carmen, the real estate agent from Miami we met in Chapter 4, had strong words about the DL dynamic from the trans woman's perspective.

"I stopped dating DL men five years ago. Not because I judge them, I understand the pressure they're under. I stopped because I was tired of being a secret. I was tired of being the most important person in someone's life on a Tuesday evening and a ghost by Wednesday morning. I was tired of being the one who had to turn off her emotions when he went home to his wife, and turn them back on when he came back. That switch, the on-and-off of it, was destroying me."

"To the wives: I know you think we have it easy. That we're getting the fun part while you get the hard work. But we get the hard work too. We just get a different kind. You get the house, the ring, the public acknowledgment. We get the passion, the vulnerability, the real him; but only in a locked room with the blinds closed. And then we get to watch him drive away. Every single time, we watch him drive away. And we sit there wondering when he'll come back and whether this will be the time he doesn't."

A Drag Queen's Perspective: Duchess

Duchess is forty-five and performs at clubs across the Southeast. She has a different relationship with DL men than the trans women and femboys in this chapter, her encounters have been shorter, more physical, less emotionally entangled. But her perspective is valuable because she sees the DL dynamic from the entertainment side.

"They come to the shows. They sit in the back, usually alone. They don't tip where people can see: they wait until after the show, find you backstage, slip you a hundred and their phone number. I've seen deacons in the audience. I've seen coaches. I've seen men I went to high school with who used to call people like me every name in the book. And now they're in my DMs at one in the morning."

"What I want the wives to know is that this is bigger than your husband. This is a culture. This is a community. This is thousands and thousands of men across this country who are living double lives because the world they were born into gave them no other option. Your husband is not an anomaly. He's a statistic. And until the culture changes, the statistics are going to keep getting worse."

The Femboys Speak

Rio: "I'm Not a Phase"

Rio is twenty-three and lives in Baltimore. We met Rio briefly in Chapter 7 as the person Keisha's boyfriend Darius was involved with. Rio agreed to share his perspective.

"The thing that hurts the most is being treated like a phase. Like I'm something he's experimenting with, something he'll grow out of, something that doesn't count because I'm not a 'real woman.' I'm a real person. I have real feelings. And when a man texts me every day for six months, tells me he cares about me, spends time with me, shares parts of himself with me, and then ghosts me the second his girlfriend gets suspicious, that's not a phase ending. That's a person being discarded."

"I know the girlfriend sees me as the problem. But I wasn't Darius's problem. I was the place where Darius felt safe enough to be honest about what he wanted. And when that place got too risky, he threw it away, threw me away, to protect his image. That's the pattern with DL men. They come to you when they need to feel free. They leave you when the freedom starts to cost them something."

Phoenix: "The Disposability Is the Cruelest Part"

Phoenix is thirty and uses they/them pronouns. They live in Los Angeles and have been involved with multiple DL men over the past several years.

"There's a specific kind of cruelty that DL men specialize in, and it's the cruelty of disposability. When they're with you, you are everything. You are beautiful. You are special. You are the only one who understands them. And then one day, maybe because his wife found something, maybe because a friend almost saw him, maybe because the guilt just got too heavy, you become nothing. Blocked. Deleted. Erased. Like you never existed. Like the six months or two years of your life you gave him were a hallucination."

"What I want the wives to know is this: we are not disposable to ourselves, even if we are disposable to your husbands. We are human beings who loved and were loved and then were thrown away when the cost of keeping us became too high. Your pain is real. But so is ours. And the man who caused both is the same man."

The DL Men Speak

Marcus: "I Am Not a Monster"

Marcus, whom we met in Chapter 5, agreed to speak at greater length for this chapter. He is thirty-seven and lives in Phoenix. His wife discovered his involvement with a trans woman in Tucson nearly two years into the relationship.

"I know what people think when they hear 'DL.' They think predator. They think liar. They think monster. And I was a liar, I'm not going to deny that. I lied every single day for two years. But I am not a monster. I am a man who was carrying something he didn't have the language for, the courage for, or the support system for. I didn't wake up one morning and decide to destroy my marriage. I woke up one morning and realized that a part of me existed that I had been suffocating for twenty years, and I didn't know how to let it breathe without burning everything down."

"What I want my wife to understand, what I want all the wives to understand, is that the deception was not about you. It was about me. About my fear. My shame. My inability to imagine a world where I could be honest about what I wanted and still keep the life I'd built. I chose to lie because I was a coward. Not because you were lacking. Not because I didn't love you. Because I was too afraid of what the truth would cost me."

Keith: "The Shame Is a Prison"

Keith, the school principal from Chapter 6, also wanted to share more for this chapter.

"The shame is a prison, and the prison is self-built. Nobody locked me in here. I built the cell with my own hands, every lie, every cover story, every time I looked my wife in the eye and told her nothing was wrong. I built it because the alternative, the truth, felt like a death sentence. If I told the truth, I would lose my job. I would lose my church. I would lose my standing in the community. I would lose my children's respect. I would lose everything I spent my entire life building. And so I kept building the cell instead. One lie at a time. Until the cell became so solid that I couldn't see a way out even if I wanted one."

"I'm not asking for sympathy. I made my choices and I will live with the consequences. But I am asking for understanding, not of the behavior, but of the conditions that produce it. Black men in this country are given no space to be sexually complex. No space to be vulnerable. No space to explore desire that doesn't fit the box. And when you give a person no space to be honest, you shouldn't be surprised when they learn to lie."

Terrance: "I Wish I Could Stop"

Terrance, from Chapter 4, has been involved with trans woman Paris for two years while maintaining his relationship with his girlfriend Yvette.

"Everybody thinks DL men are having the time of their lives. Running around, having our cake and eating it too. But I am miserable. I am exhausted from the lies. I am torn apart by the guilt. I love Yvette and I love Paris and I cannot have both and I cannot give up either and every single day I wake up and feel like I'm drowning. I'm not enjoying this. I'm surviving it. And I don't know how to stop because stopping in either direction means destroying someone I love."

"If I could go back and do it differently, if I could have grown up in a world where a Black man could say 'I am attracted to trans women' without being called gay, without being kicked out, without being shunned, I would never have needed the secret life. The secret life exists because the public life doesn't have room for what I am. And until that changes, there will be more men like me. And more women like Yvette who get hurt."

Darnell: "I Am Two People"

Darnell, the regional sales manager from Chapter 5, also shared more of his inner world for this chapter.

"I am two people. There is the Darnell who coaches his son's basketball team, who takes his daughter to dance recital, who sits in the front pew at church on Sunday. That Darnell is real. And then there is the Darnell who drives to another city twice a month to see a woman his family doesn't know exists. That Darnell is also real. And the gap between them, the no-man's-land between those two versions of me, is where I live most of my life. In the gap. In the in-between. And it is the loneliest place I have ever been."

"People think DL men have it made. Two relationships. Double the love. Double the sex. But what they don't see is the double the anxiety. Double the guilt. Double the fear. Every morning I wake up calculating, what did I say to Angela last night that I need to remember, what did I promise Imani that I need to follow through on, where am I supposed to be today, what lies have I told this week that I need to keep straight. My mind never stops. I haven't had a moment of peace in two and a half years."

"If my wife is reading this: Angela, I am sorry. Not the kind of sorry that fixes anything. The kind of sorry that acknowledges that I took something from you that I had no right to take, your ability to make an informed decision about your own life. You deserved the truth. You deserved to know who you were married to. And the fact that I didn't give you that, that I chose my fear over your freedom, is the thing I will spend the rest of my life regretting."

What Each Side Wishes You Knew

At the end of each conversation, I asked the same question: "If you could say one thing directly to the wives and girlfriends, what would it be?" Here are the answers, organized by perspective:

From the Trans Women

"We didn't steal your man. He came to us carrying a part of himself that he couldn't bring home. We received that part. Sometimes we fell in love with it. But we didn't create it and we didn't cause it.", Serena

"Your anger is valid. Direct it at the right person. We were pawns in his game too.", Diamond

"Please don't let his secret turn into your shame. You did nothing wrong. Neither did we. He did.", Carmen

"If you ever want to talk, really talk, to the woman on the other side, some of us would welcome that conversation. Not to fight. Not to compete. But to understand. We have more in common than you think.", Valentina

From the Femboys

"I'm not a phase. I'm not a fetish. I'm a human being who was loved in secret and discarded in silence. Your husband's attraction to me doesn't diminish his attraction to you. But his decision to hide it diminished us both.", Rio

"The system that hurt you is the same system that hurt us. We're not on opposite sides. We're in the same trap.", Phoenix

From the DL Men

"I am not a monster. I am a man who was too afraid to be honest. That doesn't make what I did okay. But it does make me human. And I need you to know that the lies were about my fear, not about your inadequacy.", Marcus

"If I could give you one gift, it would be the knowledge that this was never about you. You were always enough. I was the one who wasn't enough, wasn't brave enough, wasn't honest enough, wasn't strong enough to be the man you deserved. That failure is mine. Not yours.", Keith

"I wish the world would let men like me exist without shame. Not so I can keep lying, so I can stop.", Terrance

What All Three Sides Agree On

In all of the conversations I had for this chapter, across all three perspectives, certain themes emerged with striking consistency. Let me share them with you.

Everyone agrees that secrecy is the poison. Not the attraction. Not the gender identity. The secrecy. Every person I spoke with, trans woman, femboy, and DL man, identified the lying as the source of the damage. If honesty were possible, the attraction itself would simply be a feature of human sexuality. It is the necessity of hiding it that transforms it into a weapon that wounds everyone it touches.

Everyone agrees that the wife is the person who suffers most. This was unanimous and immediate. Trans women said it. Femboys said it. DL men said it. Whatever pain they themselves were carrying, every single one of them acknowledged that the woman at home: the woman who didn't know, who didn't consent, who built her life on a foundation she didn't know was fractured, bears the heaviest burden. If you have felt invisible in this dynamic, know that you are not invisible to the other people inside it. They see you. They know what this costs you. And most of them carry guilt about it.

Everyone agrees that culture is the engine. The rigid expectations of masculinity, the hostility toward sexual complexity, the moralistic frameworks that treat desire as something that must be controlled rather than understood, these are the cultural forces that produce the DL phenomenon. The men don't hide because they enjoy hiding. The trans women don't accept being secrets because they enjoy secrecy. Everyone is responding to a culture that has created impossible conditions: be yourself, but only if yourself fits within the boundaries we've drawn for you.

And everyone agrees on one final thing: something has to change. The current system, where men hide, women are deceived, and trans women and femboys are disposable, serves no one. It produces only pain. And while this book cannot single-handedly change the culture, it can do what every meaningful change begins with: it can tell the truth.

My Perspective: Standing at the Intersection

I want to step out of my role as narrator for a moment and speak personally. As an African-American person in the LGBTQIA community, I have watched this dynamic from a unique vantage point. I have been in the rooms where trans women compare DM screenshots from married men. I have been in the barbershops where men speak in code about desires they can't name out loud. I have been at the kitchen tables where women pour out their confusion and grief to someone they trust. I have seen every angle of this, and the thing that strikes me most is how much unnecessary pain is generated by a system that could, with more honesty and more compassion, work differently.

This book is not an argument for any particular outcome. I am not telling DL men to come out. I am not telling wives to stay or leave. I am not telling trans women to stop dating married men. I am telling everyone the truth about what this dynamic looks like from the inside, all sides of the inside, so that each person involved can make better-informed decisions about their own life.

But if I'm being honest, and this book has been nothing if not honest, I will say this: the pain I have witnessed is overwhelmingly the result of secrecy, not sexuality. The attraction itself, stripped of the shame and the lies, is simply a feature of human desire. Men who are attracted to femininity in all it's forms are not broken. They are not deviant. They are not sick. They are people whose desire operates on a broader spectrum than the culture currently accommodates. And until the culture accommodates it, until there is space for a man to say "I am attracted to trans women" without losing his job, his family, his standing, and his self-respect: the DL will continue to exist, and the pain it generates will continue to multiply.

I have spent a lot of time with the pain in these pages. The wives' pain. The trans women's pain. The DL men's pain. The femboys' pain. And if I could distill everything I've learned into a single sentence, it would be this: nobody in this dynamic is getting what they need, because the system was designed to prevent honesty, and without honesty, nobody's needs can be met.

The wives need honesty to make informed decisions about their lives. The DL men need honesty to stop living in the suffocating space between two realities. The trans women and femboys need honesty to stop being treated as expendable secrets. And our culture, our churches, our families, our communities, needs honesty to stop producing generation after generation of men who feel they have no choice but to lie.

A Note on Compassion

I know that asking you to feel compassion for the people on the other side of this dynamic is a big ask. You may not be there yet. That's fine. Compassion is not a requirement for healing. You can heal while still being furious at your husband, resentful of the trans woman, and indifferent to the femboy's feelings. Your emotional bandwidth is limited right now, and it should be directed first and foremost toward your own recovery.

But if and when the time comes, months or years from now, when the acute pain has subsided enough to allow some expansion of perspective, I believe that compassion will serve you. Not because the other people in this dynamic deserve your compassion, but because compassion is fundamentally an act of self-liberation. Anger, resentment, and bitterness are heavy. They take up space in your body and your mind. Compassion, not forgiveness, not acceptance, just the basic human acknowledgment that other people are also suffering, lightens the load. And you deserve to travel lighter.

You don't have to get there today. You may never get there at all, and that's your right. But the voices in this chapter were offered to you as an invitation: an invitation to see the full human landscape of a situation that your pain has understandably narrowed. When you're ready to accept that invitation, it will be here.

What Our Community Needs to Hear

I would be failing my own community if I closed this chapter without addressing the broader culture that produces this dynamic. Because the DL phenomenon is not a private matter between individuals: it is a public health crisis, a mental health crisis, and a relational crisis that affects thousands of families across the Black community and beyond.

Our churches need to hear that shaming men for their sexual desires does not make those desires disappear. It drives them underground. Every sermon that equates attraction to trans women with perversion, every Bible study that treats any deviation from rigid heterosexuality as an abomination, every whispered conversation in the church lobby that treats DL men as the ultimate sinners, these do not prevent DL behavior. They guarantee it. They guarantee that men will hide. They guarantee that wives will be deceived. They guarantee that trans women will be used and discarded. The church's approach to sexuality is producing the very outcomes it claims to oppose.

Our families need to hear that the way we raise Black boys: the rigid masculinity, the emotional suppression, the zero-tolerance policy for softness, vulnerability, or any desire that doesn't fit the approved script, is producing men who are incapable of honesty about their own inner lives. And those men grow up to be husbands who lie, because lying is the only tool they were ever given for managing the parts of themselves that don't fit the mold.

Our partners and friends need to hear that when a woman comes to you with this specific type of betrayal, she needs your compassion, not your curiosity. She doesn't need you to ask probing questions about the details. She doesn't need you to share the story at brunch. She needs you to hold her, to listen, and to remind her that she is not alone and she is not damaged. If you can't do that, be honest about your limitations and help her find someone who can.

And our men need to hear this: you are allowed to be sexually complex. You are allowed to be attracted to femininity in all it's forms. You are allowed to need softness, vulnerability, and emotional freedom. These are not weaknesses. They are human needs. And the courage to acknowledge them, to yourself and eventually to the people who share your life, is not the end of your world. It is the beginning of a world where your wife doesn't have to pick up a book like this to understand what happened to her marriage.

A Final Word

I asked each person I interviewed whether they would read this book if it existed. Every single one of them said yes; and every one of them said they wished it had existed sooner. The trans women wished it existed so that the wives could understand them as human beings rather than as threats. The femboys wished it existed so that someone, anyone, would acknowledge that they are people, not fetish objects. The DL men wished it existed so that their wives might have a framework for understanding something that feels incomprehensible without context. And the wives wished it existed for the most basic reason of all: because when you are going through the worst experience of your life, there is nothing more isolating than believing nobody has ever been through it before.

You are not alone. None of you are. The walls between the people in this dynamic are built of secrecy and shame, and those walls make everyone feel isolated. But on the other side of every wall is another human being who is also in pain, also confused, also wishing things were different. This chapter was my attempt to lower those walls just enough for you to see each other. Not to reconcile. Not to embrace. Just to see.

Because seeing is the first step toward everything that comes next.

This chapter was the hardest one to write, because it required me to hold space for everyone's pain simultaneously, without ranking it, without choosing sides, without letting any one perspective dominate. If you read it and feel confused, that's okay. If you read it and feel angry, that's okay too. If you read it and felt a flicker of empathy you didn't expect, for Serena sitting alone on Christmas, for Rio being ghosted after six months of daily texts, for Marcus drowning in his own shame, for Darnell calculating his lies before breakfast, let that flicker live. It doesn't diminish your pain. It enlarges your understanding. And understanding is the foundation on which every good decision is built.

I chose to include this chapter in the book not because the other voices deserve equal billing with yours. They don't. You are the person this book was written for. But your ability to move forward, to make the best decision for your life, depends on having a complete picture of what you're moving forward from. And a complete picture requires seeing beyond your own pain, if only for a moment, to understand the ecosystem that produced it.

Serena, Diamond, Carmen, Valentina, Duchess, Rio, Phoenix, Marcus, Keith, Terrance, Darnell, these voices exist in conversation with the voices of Sandra, Patricia, Nicole, Denise, Keisha, Francine, Tamara, and every other woman whose story has filled these pages. Together, they form the complete portrait of a dynamic that has been shrouded in silence for too long. And silence, as we've established throughout this book, is the soil that the secret life grows in. The more light we bring, the less room the secret has to survive.

The next chapter, the final full chapter, is about your decision. Staying, leaving, or evolving. Three paths, no judgment, and every resource I can give you to help you choose the one that's right for your life. You've earned that chapter. You've done the hard work of understanding. Now it's time to decide.

CHAPTER ELEVEN

Staying, Leaving, or Evolving: Making Your Decision

You have done something remarkable. You have read ten chapters of information that most people would flinch away from. You have looked at the psychology, the science, the money, the apps, the emotional terrain, the health risks, and the voices from all sides of a dynamic that most of our culture pretends doesn't exist. You did that because you are a woman who values truth over comfort. And now, armed with that truth, you face the decision that all of this has been leading to: What do I do now?

I am going to present three paths. Not two, three. Because the binary of "stay or leave" does not capture the full range of options available to you. The three paths are: staying and rebuilding, leaving and starting over, and evolving the relationship into something different than it was before. Each path has its own requirements, its own risks, and its own version of healing. None of them is easy. None of them is painless. And none of them is wrong.

I am not going to tell you which path to choose. That decision belongs to you and you alone. What I am going to do is give you the clearest possible picture of what each path looks like, what it requires, what it costs, what it offers, so that your decision is informed by reality, not by fear, not by shame, and not by the pressure of anyone else's expectations.

Path One: Staying and Rebuilding

Let's start with the path that will attract the most judgment from others and the most internal conflict within you. Staying. Choosing to remain in the marriage or relationship after discovering your partner's secret life. The outside world will have opinions about this choice. Some people will call you strong. Others will call you foolish. Both are projecting their own values onto your situation. Your reasons for staying are your own, and they are valid regardless of what anyone else thinks.

Women stay for many reasons: love that persists despite the betrayal, children who need stability, financial realities that make separation impossible or devastating, religious convictions about the permanence of marriage, the belief that the relationship can be repaired with honesty and work, or simply the recognition that the life they've built is worth fighting for even after it has been damaged. All of these are legitimate reasons. None of them require justification to anyone but yourself.

What Staying Requires

Staying is not the same as pretending nothing happened. If you choose to stay, the relationship must be rebuilt on a fundamentally different foundation than the one it was on before. The old foundation, where he hid and you unknowingly accepted a partial truth, is gone. It cannot be restored. What replaces it must be built on complete honesty, genuine accountability, and ongoing work from both of you.

His requirements are significant. He must end the secret relationship completely, not gradually, not "over time," but now. He must disclose the full scope of what happened, not a trickle of truth released over months as you discover more, but a complete, voluntary accounting. Trickle truth, where he admits only what you already know and reveals additional information only when confronted with evidence, is not accountability. It is continued manipulation. He must enter individual therapy with a provider who specializes in sexuality, identity, and compulsive behavior. He must agree to couples therapy with a provider you both trust. And he must demonstrate, through sustained action over time, that the deception is over.

Your requirements are equally important. You must be willing to engage in the rebuilding process authentically, not as a surveillance operation where you monitor his every move, but as a genuine effort to reconstruct trust. This does not mean being naïve. Verification is reasonable, especially in the early stages. But if you find yourself unable to move past the role of investigator, checking his phone daily, tracking his location, interrogating him about every absence: that is a sign that the trust damage may be too severe for the relationship to survive. Trust yourself to recognize that limit if it arrives.

Finding the Right Therapist for Couples Work

The therapist you choose for couples work will significantly impact the outcome. In this specific situation, you need a therapist who has experience with three distinct areas: infidelity and betrayal recovery, LGBTQ-inclusive or affirmative practice, and complex male sexuality including attraction to trans and gender-diverse individuals. If the therapist treats the gender identity element as the primary pathology, "he's clearly gay and in denial", that therapist will not serve your situation well. If the therapist minimizes the betrayal because the attraction is "just part of who he is": that therapist will not serve you well either. You need someone who can hold both the betrayal and the sexuality simultaneously, without privileging either.

Ask directly during the initial consultation: "Do you have experience working with couples where one partner has been involved with a transgender individual?" If the answer is no, or if the therapist seems uncomfortable with the question, keep looking. The Gottman Institute's directory, the American Association of Sexuality Educators, Counselors, and Therapists, and Psychology Today's therapist finder all allow you to filter by specialty. Use those tools.

What Genuine Accountability Looks Like

This is critical, because many DL men, when confronted, will perform remorse without actually being remorseful. The performance looks like tears, apologies, promises to change, and immediate over-attentiveness. Genuine accountability looks different. It is sustained, not performative. It shows up in the small daily choices, transparency with his phone, honesty about his whereabouts, willingness to answer your questions without becoming defensive, not just in the dramatic gestures.

Genuine accountability includes the willingness to sit in your pain without trying to fix it or rush you through it. If he says, "How long are you going to punish me for this?" or "We need to move on," he is prioritizing his comfort over your healing. That is a red flag. Healing takes as long as it takes, and a man who is genuinely accountable will hold space for your process without imposing a timeline.

Genuine accountability also includes the willingness to explore, honestly and without defensiveness, his own sexuality. Not to pathologize it or cure it, but to understand it. A man who is attracted to trans women and who wants to rebuild his marriage needs to understand his own desire well enough to make an informed commitment about how he will manage it going forward. That understanding requires therapeutic work, not conversion therapy, not suppression, but honest exploration of who he is and what he needs.

Francine's Path

Francine, from Chapter 8, chose to stay. Eight years later, she described the rebuilding process with unflinching honesty.

"The first two years were hell. I don't use that word lightly. We were in therapy twice a week, once individually, once together. There were nights I screamed at him until my voice was gone. There were weeks he slept in the guest room. There were moments I was absolutely certain I was going to leave. But I didn't. And the reason I didn't was not because I'm a saint or because I'm weak. It's because underneath the rage and the grief, there was still a relationship worth saving. Not the old relationship: that one was dead. A new one. Built on a truth that the old one never had."

"Robert is a different man now. Not because he stopped being attracted to trans women: he didn't. That's part of who he is and it's not going to change. But he stopped lying about it. He stopped hiding. We talk about it openly now, his desires, his temptations, what he's feeling. And that openness, as uncomfortable as it sometimes is, has created an intimacy in our marriage that we never had before. The marriage we have now is more honest than the one we had for the first twenty years. I wouldn't have chosen this path. But since I'm on it, I'm grateful for where it led."

Path Two: Leaving and Starting Over

For many women, leaving is the right decision. Not the easy decision, there is nothing easy about dissolving a marriage or ending a long-term relationship, especially when children, finances, and community are involved. But for some women, the betrayal is a line that, once crossed, cannot be uncrossed. And the discovery that their partner's secret life involved trans women or femboys adds a dimension that makes staying feel impossible, not because of judgment toward the trans community, but because the scope of the deception is too vast to rebuild from.

If this is where you are, honor that. You are not giving up. You are not weak. You are not failing. You are choosing yourself. You are saying, "This is more than I can carry and still be whole," and that is one of the bravest things a person can say.

Practical Considerations

Before you leave, protect yourself. Consult with a family law attorney, ideally before you have the final conversation with your partner, to understand your rights regarding property, assets, spousal support, and custody. Gather financial documents: tax returns, bank statements, investment accounts, retirement accounts, property deeds. If you share finances, open your own bank account and begin establishing financial independence. These are not aggressive actions: they are protective ones.

If children are involved, the conversation about custody needs to be handled with particular care. Your children need to be protected from the details of their father's secret life, at least until they are old enough to process the information without being traumatized by it. A skilled family therapist can help you determine age-appropriate disclosures and navigate co-parenting in the aftermath of a complex betrayal.

Think carefully about what you share with others. You will need support during the separation, but you do not need to disclose the specific nature of his infidelity to everyone. You can say, "The marriage is ending due to infidelity and a fundamental breach of trust," without specifying the details. Share the full story only with the people you trust completely and who need to know, your therapist, your attorney, and perhaps one or two close confidants.

Nicole's Path

Nicole, the accountant from Chapter 5 who discovered her husband Raymond's eleven thousand dollars in payments to a trans woman named Bianca, chose to leave. She described her decision-making process as a mathematical one, which made sense given her professional background.

"I sat down and ran the numbers," Nicole told me. "Not just the financial numbers, though those were damning, but the emotional numbers. How much trust was left? Zero. How much willingness did he show to be fully honest? Minimal, I had to drag every admission out of him. How much of our relationship was built on a foundation that still existed? Not enough. The math didn't work. And I'm an accountant. I know what it looks like when the numbers don't add up."

"Leaving was terrifying. We had been together for fourteen years. Shared everything. But I realized that what I was really afraid of wasn't being alone: it was starting over. And starting over, as scary as it sounded, was better than staying in a life that was built on a lie. I filed for divorce six months after the discovery. It was finalized eight months after that. And the morning I signed those papers, I felt something I hadn't felt in over a year: relief."

The Emotional Dimension of Leaving

I want to be honest about what leaving feels like, because the cultural narrative often presents it as empowerment, "she left, she's strong, she's free." And eventually, it may feel that way. But in the immediate aftermath, leaving often feels like dying. You are not just ending a relationship. You are dismantling a life. The home you shared, the routines you built, the future you planned, the identity you held as a wife, all of it is being taken apart, piece by piece. And each piece hurts.

There will be days when you question your decision. Days when you miss him so intensely that you almost call. Days when you see a family at the park and the grief hits you like a wall. These days are not evidence that you made the wrong choice. They are evidence that you loved someone deeply and that love doesn't evaporate just because trust does. The grief of leaving is the grief of love that was real, even though the relationship was not what you thought. Let yourself grieve. Don't let anyone tell you that leaving should feel triumphant. It will feel triumphant eventually. First, it will feel terrible. That's normal.

What sustains you through the terrible is purpose: the knowledge that you chose this path because you deserve a life built on truth. Every morning you wake up in your new space, even if that space is smaller or lonelier than what you left behind, is a morning you wake up free. Free from the lies. Free from the surveillance. Free from the corrosive anxiety of wondering what else you don't know. That freedom is priceless, even when it's painful.

Recognizing Manipulation: When Staying Is Not a Choice but a Trap

Before you make any decision, I need to warn you about manipulation tactics that DL men, like all unfaithful partners, may deploy to prevent you from leaving. Recognizing these tactics is essential to ensuring that whatever you choose, you choose it freely.

Gaslighting: He may try to make you doubt your own perception. "You're making this into something it's not." "It was just a friendship." "You're being paranoid." If you have evidence, screenshots, messages, financial records, your perception is not the problem. His honesty is.

Love bombing: In the aftermath of discovery, he may become the most attentive, loving partner you've ever seen. Flowers. Surprise dates. Constant affirmation. This can feel like genuine remorse, but if it started the moment he was caught and not before, it is more likely a strategy to keep you from leaving. Genuine change is sustained and shows up in accountability, not in grand gestures.

Weaponizing the children: "Think about what this will do to the kids." This statement, while emotionally powerful, is designed to make you feel responsible for the consequences of his actions. He created this situation. If the family is disrupted, it is because of his choices, not your response to them.

Threats of self-harm: Some men, when cornered, will threaten to hurt themselves if you leave. This is a manipulation tactic, and it is a serious one. If he threatens self-harm, take it seriously by contacting appropriate resources, but do not let it be the reason you stay. His emotional well-being is not your hostage to manage. If he is genuinely in crisis, a mental health professional can help him. You are not his therapist. You are his wife, and your first obligation is to yourself.

The promise of change without evidence: "I'll never do it again." "I'm done with that life." "It's over." Words without corresponding action are just more lies dressed in better clothing. If he says he's changed, the proof is in what he does, not what he says: Is he in therapy? Has he ended all contact? Is he transparent with his phone and his schedule? Is he willing to do the sustained, unglamorous work of rebuilding trust? If the answer to any of these is no, the promise is empty.

Path Three: Evolving the Relationship

The third path is the one that most people don't consider, because our culture doesn't have a well-established framework for it. Evolving the relationship means staying together but fundamentally renegotiating the terms of the partnership. This can take many forms, and what it looks like depends entirely on what both of you are willing to accept.

For some couples, evolution means an open or partially open relationship: an arrangement where the man is permitted to explore his attraction to trans women or femboys within agreed-upon boundaries, while the marriage remains intact. This is not for everyone, and it requires an extraordinary level of communication, trust, and emotional maturity from both partners. But for couples where the love is strong, where the betrayal was about the secrecy rather than the attraction itself, and where the wife is able to separate her self-worth from her partner's sexual desire, this path can work.

For other couples, evolution means a redefined partnership that is no longer sexual or romantic but remains a collaborative co-parenting and financial arrangement. The marriage continues as a legal and practical structure, but both partners acknowledge that the romantic dimension has fundamentally changed. This is more common than people realize, particularly among couples with deep financial entanglement, strong religious commitments, or children who benefit from an intact family structure.

For still others, evolution means a gradual, planned transition toward separation, not a sudden, crisis-driven divorce but a thoughtful, mutually agreed-upon process that allows both partners to prepare financially, emotionally, and logistically. This path removes the urgency and the chaos and replaces it with a plan. And plans, as any woman who has survived a crisis knows, are how you take back control.

What Evolution Requires

All forms of evolution require one thing above all else: his complete honesty about who he is and what he needs. If he is still hiding, still minimizing, still telling you what he thinks you want to hear rather than the truth, no form of evolution is possible. Evolution requires two people standing in full daylight, seeing each other clearly, and deciding together what kind of partnership is sustainable given the full picture. If he cannot stand in that daylight, you are left with only two paths: staying in the darkness with him, or leaving it behind.

Evolution also requires you to do something that may feel counterintuitive: release the expectation that the relationship will return to what it was before. It won't. The relationship as you knew it ended the moment the secret was revealed. What you are building now is something new; and what's new can only emerge if you stop trying to restore what was old. This is not giving up. It is growing up. It is the recognition that life does not always follow the script we wrote, and that revising the script is sometimes braver than clinging to it.

Michelle's Unexpected Evolution

Michelle, the nurse from Chapter 8, chose a form of evolution that she never expected. After months of therapy and honest conversations with her husband DeShawn, they arrived at an arrangement that defied every expectation she had for her marriage but that, she said, ultimately saved both of them.

"DeShawn told me the truth: that his attraction to trans women was not going away. That he had tried to suppress it for his entire adult life and that the suppression was what led to the secret life. He said he loved me and wanted to stay, but he could not promise to never act on the attraction again if it meant returning to the cycle of shame and secrecy."

"We spent four months in couples therapy working through what an honest relationship could look like. What we landed on was an arrangement with strict boundaries: he could, with my knowledge and within agreed-upon rules, explore that part of himself. In return, I got something I had never had in our marriage, complete honesty. No more wondering. No more surveillance. No more lying in bed calculating whether his story added up. I know where he is. I know who he's with. And I have the power to renegotiate or end the arrangement at any time."

"Is this what I imagined for my marriage? No. Not even close. But is it better than the alternative, him hiding, me investigating, both of us drowning? Yes. By a mile. This arrangement requires more trust, not less. More communication, not less. More courage, not less. It's the hardest thing I've ever agreed to. And it's the most honest relationship I've ever been in."

I want to be clear: Michelle's path is not for everyone. Many women will read her story and feel repulsed by the very idea. That is a completely valid response. I include her story not as a recommendation but as evidence that the range of possible outcomes is wider than the culture suggests. Your life does not have to fit into a box that someone else designed. It only has to fit you.

Regardless of Which Path You Choose

Some things are true no matter which path you take. Let me lay them out:

Take your time. You do not have to decide today. You do not have to decide this month. Major life decisions made in the aftermath of trauma are almost never the best decisions you could make. Give yourself at least six months of therapy and processing before committing to any irreversible course of action. The only exception is if your physical safety is at risk, in which case you should remove yourself immediately.

Get individual therapy regardless. Whether you stay, leave, or evolve, you need your own therapeutic space to process this experience. Couples therapy is for the relationship. Individual therapy is for you. Both are necessary, but if you can only afford one, choose the individual therapy. Your healing is the non-negotiable.

Protect your finances. Regardless of your decision, establish financial independence if you don't already have it. Open your own bank account. Understand your household's full financial picture. Know what you're entitled to. Financial dependence is one of the most common reasons women stay in situations that are no longer serving them. Don't let money be the reason you can't choose freely.

Set boundaries and enforce them. Whatever you decide, the new normal must include boundaries that protect your well-being. If you stay: boundaries around transparency, communication, and accountability. If you leave: boundaries around co-parenting, financial dealings, and communication. If you evolve: boundaries around what is and isn't acceptable within the new arrangement. Boundaries without enforcement are just wishes. Enforce them.

Do not let anyone else's opinion determine your path. Your mother, your pastor, your best friend, the voices on social media, none of them have to live with your decision. You do. Make the decision that is right for your life, your circumstances, and your values. The people who love you will support whatever you choose. The people who don't support it are showing you where their loyalty actually lies.

Creating Your Timeline: How Long Should You Take?

There is no universal timeline for making this decision. What I can tell you is what the research on betrayal recovery and the experiences of women I've spoken with suggest as a reasonable framework.

The first zero to three months after discovery is crisis mode. During this phase, your brain is in survival mode. You are not thinking clearly, and that is normal. This is not the time to make permanent decisions. This is the time to stabilize: get tested, find a therapist, secure the evidence, confide in one trusted person, and take care of your physical health. Your only job in this phase is to survive and to stop the bleeding.

Three to six months is the processing phase. The acute shock has subsided enough for you to think more clearly. You are in therapy. You are learning to separate the shame from the truth. You are beginning to see the situation with some perspective. This is when many women begin to have a sense of which direction they are leaning; but the leaning is still fluid. Let it be fluid. Don't lock yourself into a decision during this phase if you can avoid it.

Six months to one year is the decision window. By this point, you have processed the initial trauma, you have gathered information, you have observed his behavior since the discovery, and you have a clearer picture of what you can and cannot live with. Most women I've spoken with who are satisfied with their decisions made them during this window, not in the first weeks, and not after years of agonizing, but in the period where the acute pain had passed and the clarity had arrived.

Beyond one year: if you have been sitting with the decision for more than a year without being able to commit to any path, that indecision itself may be a sign that you need more support: a different therapist, a trial separation, or a structured decision-making process facilitated by a professional. Chronic indecision is a form of suffering, and you deserve to be released from it.

Sandra's Path

Sandra, from Chapter 6, whose husband Wendell's three-year emotional relationship with Jade was revealed through Facebook screenshots, chose to leave. But her path to that decision was not linear.

"I went back and forth for nine months," Sandra told me. "One week I was ready to file. The next week I was thinking maybe we could work it out. The week after that I couldn't get out of bed. My therapist finally said something that changed everything. She said, 'Sandra, you keep asking yourself whether you can forgive him. That's not the right question. The right question is: Can you trust him again? Forgiveness is about the past. Trust is about the future. And you're the only one who knows whether you can build a future with someone whose past looks like this.'"

"That question clarified everything. Could I forgive him? Maybe. Eventually. With enough time and therapy. But could I trust him? Every time I imagined lying next to him at night, wondering if he was texting Jade, wondering if there was another Jade I didn't know about, I knew. I could not trust him. And a marriage without trust is a house without a foundation. Beautiful on the outside. Collapsing on the inside."

"I filed for divorce at the ten-month mark. It was the hardest thing I've ever done. But it was also the truest thing I've ever done. I chose a life I could live honestly in. And that's all any of us can do."

A Word About the Children

If you have children, they are a factor in your decision; but they should not be the factor. "Staying together for the kids" is a cultural narrative that sounds noble but can be harmful if the environment you're staying in is one of tension, resentment, and unresolved pain. Children are extraordinarily perceptive. They can feel the difference between a home where the parents genuinely love each other and a home where the parents are performing love while dying inside.

What children need most is not an intact family structure: it is emotional safety, honest communication at age-appropriate levels, and parents who are healthy enough to show up for them. If staying allows you to provide that: stay. If leaving allows you to provide that: leave. If evolving allows you to provide that: evolve. The question is not "What does an intact family look like?" The question is "What does a healthy environment for my children look like?" And only you can answer that.

If you do separate, your children will have questions. They will want to know why Daddy doesn't live here anymore. They will want to know if it's their fault. They will want to know if you still love each other. Have answers prepared that are honest but age-appropriate. "Mommy and Daddy are going to live in different houses, but we both love you exactly the same" is sufficient for young children. Adolescents may need slightly more: "Daddy made some choices that hurt our family, and we're working through what that means." The details, the trans woman, the femboy, the secret life, are not for children. They are for adults to process. Protect your children from the specifics until they are old enough to handle them, and let a family therapist guide you on when and how that conversation should happen.

If you stay or evolve, your children will also have questions, perhaps not now, but eventually. Children who grow up in homes where the emotional temperature shifted dramatically, where Mom and Dad went through something they can sense but can't name, often ask questions later, as teenagers or adults. Be prepared for that. The same therapist who helped you navigate the crisis can help you prepare for the day your grown child asks, "What happened between you and Dad when I was ten?"

Tamara's Decision

Tamara, from Chapter 6, chose the evolution path. After discovering her husband Earl's five-year emotional relationship with Simone, Tamara spent a year in therapy before making any decision. When she was ready, she and Earl sat down with their therapist and had the most honest conversation of their twenty-seven-year marriage.

"We decided that our marriage was going to look different from now on," Tamara told me. "Not open, I wasn't comfortable with that. But different. Earl agreed to complete transparency. No more secrets. No more hidden phones. And he agreed to explore, in therapy, what he actually needs to be healthy and whole. I agreed to stop punishing him and to start building something new with him. Not because he deserved grace: he didn't. But because I deserved to stop living in the wreckage."

"Our marriage today is not what it was five years ago. It is quieter. More careful. More honest. We have conversations now that we never would have had before, about desire, about fear, about what we actually need from each other versus what we assumed we needed. It's not perfect. Some days it's not even good. But it's real. And after twenty-seven years of something that wasn't fully real, I'll take real, even when real is hard."

Whatever you choose, know this: the decision is yours. Not his. Not your mother's. Not your pastor's. Yours. You have earned the right to make it by doing the hardest work a person can do, looking at a painful truth and choosing to understand it rather than run from it. That understanding is your power now. Use it to build whatever comes next.

The final chapter of this book is about moving forward. Regardless of which path you choose, you will need to rebuild, your sense of self, your trust in your own judgment, your vision for your future. That chapter is a love letter to the woman you are becoming. The woman who walked through fire and came out the other side not unburned, but unbroken. The woman who chose truth when lies were easier. The woman who chose herself when everything in the culture was telling her to choose him.

That woman is you. And she is extraordinary. Let's close this book together.

CHAPTER TWELVE

Moving Forward: Reclaiming Your Power and Your Story

You made it. Twelve chapters of truth that most people don't have the courage to read, let alone live through. And yet here you are, still standing, still reading, still choosing to face this instead of running from it. That, more than anything else in this book, is the evidence of who you are. You are a woman who can survive the worst truth of her life and come out the other side asking not "Why did this happen to me?" but "What do I do now?"

This final chapter is for the "now." Not the crisis. Not the discovery. Not the decision. The now that comes after all of that: the long, quiet, daily work of reclaiming the life that was disrupted by someone else's choices. This chapter is about rebuilding trust, not in him, but in yourself. It's about setting boundaries that protect you going forward. It's about rewriting the story of your life so that this chapter, this painful, unwanted chapter, becomes a turning point rather than a tombstone. And it's about something bigger than your individual experience: it's about the culture that made all of this possible, and what each of us can do to change it.

Rebuilding Trust in Yourself

This is where the real work begins. Because the deepest wound of this experience is not the wound your partner inflicted on your relationship. It is the wound you inflicted on yourself: the loss of trust in your own judgment. If I didn't see this coming, the inner voice says, how can I trust myself to see anything coming? If I was fooled for years, how can I trust my instincts ever again? If I chose a man who was capable of this, what does that say about my ability to choose?

Let me answer those questions directly. You didn't see this coming because you weren't supposed to. He designed the deception to be invisible. Your failure to detect a lie that was engineered to be undetectable is not a failure of your judgment: it is a testament to the sophistication of his deception. Your instincts were not wrong. In fact, as we discussed in Chapter 7, many women report that their instincts were sounding alarms long before the evidence arrived. The problem was not that your instincts failed. The problem was that the culture trained you to dismiss them: "You're overreacting." "You're being insecure." "Stop being paranoid." Those messages silenced a gut that was trying to protect you.

Going forward, your job is to listen to that gut. Not to become hypervigilant or paranoid: that is the trauma talking, and it will ease with time and therapy. But to genuinely respect the signals your body and mind send you about the people and situations in your life. Your intuition is not broken. It was overridden. The difference is critical. A broken compass needs to be replaced. An overridden compass just needs to be trusted again.

Start small. Trust yourself with minor decisions. Notice when your gut tells you something about a person or a situation, and follow up on it. Over time, as you accumulate evidence that your instincts are reliable, the trust rebuilds. It doesn't happen overnight. But it happens. Every woman I've spoken with who is on the other side of this experience has told me the same thing: her instincts are sharper now than they ever were before. Not because the pain gave her superpowers, but because the pain taught her to stop dismissing the powers she already had.

Setting Boundaries That Protect Your Future

One of the most valuable things to emerge from this experience, if you allow it, is a fundamental recalibration of your boundaries. Before this, you may have had boundaries that were flexible, negotiable, or poorly defined. After this, you have the right, and the responsibility, to define boundaries that are clear, firm, and non-negotiable.

In future relationships, whether romantic, friendly, or professional, you now know what you will and will not tolerate. You will not tolerate a partner who is secretive with their phone. You will not tolerate unexplained absences. You will not tolerate financial opacity. You will not tolerate being made to feel crazy for asking reasonable questions. These are not demands born of paranoia. They are standards born of experience. And anyone who treats your standards as unreasonable is someone who benefits from your compliance.

But boundaries are not just about what you will not accept. They are also about what you insist upon: open communication, mutual transparency, emotional honesty, and the freedom to ask questions without being punished for asking. These are the conditions of a healthy relationship, and you should never again settle for less. You have paid the tuition for this lesson in the most expensive currency there is, pain. Don't waste what it taught you.

Vetting Future Partners: What You Know Now

If you are entering or considering new relationships, you carry something that most women do not: a highly developed ability to read behavioral patterns. You know what secrecy looks like. You know what compartmentalization feels like. You know the difference between a man who is private and a man who is hiding. This knowledge is not baggage: it is armor.

In future relationships, trust should be built incrementally, not assumed. Watch how a potential partner handles his phone, his schedule, his communication. Observe whether his stories are consistent. Notice whether he becomes defensive when you ask normal questions. Pay attention to how he talks about his past relationships, does he take responsibility, or does he paint himself as the perpetual victim? These are data points, and you now know how to read them.

And do not be afraid to ask direct questions. "Are you attracted to anyone other than cisgender women?" is a question you have every right to ask. His answer may or may not be honest, but his reaction to the question, whether he engages openly or becomes hostile and dismissive, will tell you a great deal about his capacity for the kind of transparency you now require.

One practical tool that several women recommended to me: before committing to a serious relationship, ask your potential partner to share their social media accounts with you, not in a surveillance way, but as a gesture of mutual transparency. A man with nothing to hide will shrug and hand over his phone. A man who reacts with outrage, deflection, or a lecture about "privacy" is telling you something important. Privacy is reasonable. Secrecy is a red flag. And after what you've been through, you know the difference.

The Importance of Continued Therapy

I have recommended therapy throughout this book, and I want to close by making the case one more time. Therapy is not a sign of weakness. It is not a luxury. It is the single most effective tool for processing betrayal trauma, rebuilding self-trust, and ensuring that the patterns of the past do not repeat in the future. And the therapy you need now may be different from the therapy you needed in the acute crisis phase.

In the early months, therapy focused on stabilization: managing the shock, processing the grief, preventing the trauma from consuming your daily functioning. That work was essential. But as you move further from the crisis, the therapeutic work shifts. It becomes about integration: weaving the experience into your life story in a way that doesn't define you but informs you. It becomes about pattern recognition: understanding not just what happened, but what in your own history may have made you vulnerable to dismissing the warning signs. Not to blame you, never to blame you, but to build a more complete understanding of yourself that protects you going forward.

And it becomes about post-traumatic growth. This is a term psychologists use to describe the phenomenon where individuals who have survived trauma develop greater psychological resilience, deeper empathy, clearer priorities, and a stronger sense of personal strength than they had before the trauma occurred. Post-traumatic growth is not inevitable: it requires intentional work, usually with professional support. But when it happens, it transforms the worst experience of your life into the foundation of a stronger, more authentic self.

If you stopped therapy after the acute phase, consider going back. If you never started, start now. If your current therapist doesn't feel like the right fit anymore, maybe you've outgrown the crisis-mode therapist and need someone who specializes in growth and identity work, give yourself permission to switch. Therapy is not a one-size-fits-all proposition. Find the therapist who meets you where you are now, not where you were six months ago.

Your Body's Healing

Throughout this book, we have talked about the physical toll of betrayal trauma: the insomnia, the weight changes, the elevated cortisol, the weakened immune system, the muscle tension, the stomach problems. As you move forward, your body needs healing just as much as your mind does.

Reestablish routines that nurture your physical self. Sleep is the foundation, if you are still struggling with insomnia, address it aggressively with your doctor. Movement helps: walking, yoga, swimming, dancing, anything that gets your body moving and reminds it that it is capable of something other than crisis. Nutrition matters: the grief may have disrupted your eating patterns, and restoring them is an act of self-care that has cascading effects on your mood, your energy, and your cognitive clarity.

Pay particular attention to your nervous system. Betrayal trauma often leaves the nervous system stuck in a state of hyperarousal, your body is still scanning for threats even when the acute danger has passed. Somatic therapies, breathwork, meditation, and progressive muscle relaxation can help recalibrate your nervous system over time. Your body held the stress of this experience for months or years. It deserves intentional help in releasing it.

Many women I spoke with found that reconnecting with physical pleasure, not sexual pleasure, but the simple pleasures of the body, was a crucial part of their recovery. A warm bath. A massage. The feeling of sun on skin. Good food, savored slowly. Dancing in the kitchen. These are not indulgences. They are acts of reclamation. Your body was a site of violation, not because of what he did to it directly, but because his choices put it at risk without your consent. Reclaiming physical pleasure is a way of telling your body: you are mine again. You are not his collateral damage. You are my home, and I am going to take care of you.

And sleep. I cannot emphasize this enough. If you are still not sleeping well months after the discovery, this is not something to push through. Chronic sleep deprivation impairs judgment, weakens immunity, intensifies anxiety, and makes it nearly impossible to think clearly about the decisions in front of you. Talk to your doctor. Consider sleep-specific therapy such as cognitive behavioral therapy for insomnia, which is highly effective and does not rely on medication. Your decision-making ability is directly correlated with the quality of your sleep. Give yourself the best possible foundation by prioritizing rest.

Lynn's Transformation

Lynn, from Chapter 8, the woman from Raleigh who made the list of things that were true about her, shared an update about her life two years after the discovery.

"I ran my first full marathon eight months after the discovery," Lynn told me. "Not because I was a runner. I wasn't. I had never run more than a mile in my life. I started running because I needed to put the rage somewhere. I needed to move the pain through my body instead of letting it sit in my chest. And somewhere around mile ten of my training, something shifted. The running stopped being about the pain and started being about me. About what my body could do. About what I was capable of when I stopped defining myself by what he did and started defining myself by what I could do."

"Crossing that finish line was the first time since the discovery that I felt genuinely proud of myself. Not proud in a coping way. Proud in a 'look what I built' way. And I realized that the same energy that got me through twenty-six miles, the stubbornness, the refusal to quit, the willingness to be uncomfortable, was the same energy that got me through the worst year of my life. I didn't discover that energy in the crisis. It was always there. The crisis just showed me what it could do."

Denitra's New Chapter

Denitra, from Chapter 8, the woman from Cleveland who set down the shame in front of her bathroom mirror, shared an update about her life three years after discovery. She left her marriage, completed two years of intensive therapy, and eventually began dating again.

"The first man I dated after my divorce, I scared him off in about three weeks," Denitra said, laughing. "I was so vigilant. Checking everything. Reading into every text. I realized I wasn't ready. I went back to therapy for another six months, worked on separating my trauma response from my actual instincts, and then tried again."

"The second time, I met a man named Charles. On our third date, I told him, not everything, but enough. I said, 'I went through something in my marriage that makes trust very important to me. I need a partner who is transparent. If that's not you, tell me now and we'll save each other the time.' And Charles looked at me and said, 'I respect that. Ask me anything.' And he meant it. That's when I knew the difference between a man who hides and a man who doesn't. It's in how they respond to the request for openness. Charles didn't flinch. And that told me everything."

"We've been together fourteen months now. Is it perfect? No. Am I still sometimes triggered? Yes. But the foundation is different this time. It's built on truth from the first brick. And that makes all the difference."

Turning Pain into Purpose

Some women who go through this experience discover, on the other side of the pain, a desire to help other women who are walking the same path. This is not a requirement of healing, you do not owe your pain to anyone, but for those who feel called to it, advocacy and support work can be profoundly transformative.

You might consider mentoring other women who are navigating similar discoveries. The isolation of this experience is one of its most damaging features, and knowing that someone else has been through it and survived can be a lifeline. You don't need professional credentials to sit with another woman and say, "I understand. I've been there. You're going to make it." Sometimes those words are more powerful than anything a therapist can offer.

You might consider contributing to the broader cultural conversation about male sexuality, honesty in relationships, and the harm caused by rigid gender expectations. Writing. Speaking. Sharing your story, on your own terms, in your own time, to the extent that feels safe. Every woman who tells her truth makes it easier for the next woman to recognize hers. And every honest conversation about the DL dynamic makes it harder for the secrecy to survive.

Or you might simply carry your experience as private wisdom, something that informs your life, your choices, and your relationships without being broadcast to the world. Not every wound needs to become a platform. Some wounds become quiet strength. Both paths are valid. Both are forms of power.

Rewriting Your Story

Right now, the story of your life has a chapter you didn't write: a chapter imposed on you by someone else's choices. And that chapter, in the raw aftermath of discovery, can feel like it has overtaken your entire narrative. You are no longer the woman who did this or accomplished that. You are the woman whose husband was involved with a trans woman. That label threatens to define you, to shrink you, to reduce the vastness of who you are to a single, devastating fact about someone else's behavior.

Refuse that reduction. You are the author of your life, and this is one chapter, not the whole book. The chapters that came before this one, your education, your career, your friendships, your accomplishments, your joys, those are still part of your story. They are still yours. And the chapters that come after this one, the rebuilding, the growth, the new relationships, the reclaimed confidence, those will be written by you, in your voice, on your terms.

Narrative therapy, a form of therapy that focuses on the stories we tell about our lives, can be particularly useful at this stage. A narrative therapist helps you identify the dominant story, "I am a woman who was betrayed", and explore alternative stories that are equally true but less confining: "I am a woman who survived betrayal and became stronger." "I am a woman who chose truth when lies were easier." "I am a woman who refused to let someone else's choices define her worth." These are not affirmations or wishful thinking. They are reinterpretations of your experience that give you agency over your own narrative.

The story you tell about yourself matters. It shapes how you see your future, how you present yourself to the world, and how you move through your days. If the story is "I was destroyed by this," your life will reflect destruction. If the story is "I was tested by this and I passed," your life will reflect strength. You get to choose which story to tell. That is perhaps the most powerful choice you will make in this entire process.

Keisha's Rewrite

Keisha, the twenty-nine-year-old from Baltimore we met in Chapter 7, shared how she rewrote her story after the discovery about Darius and Rio.

"For the first three months, my story was: 'I'm the girl whose boyfriend was seeing a femboy.' That was it. That was my whole identity. I couldn't think about anything else. I couldn't talk about anything else. I was consumed."

"My therapist asked me to write my story in three versions. The first was the victim version: everything that happened to me. The second was the survivor version: everything I did in response. And the third was the hero version: the woman I was becoming because of what I went through. Same events. Three completely different stories. And when I read the hero version out loud, I cried, not from grief, but from recognition. That woman was me. She had always been me. I just couldn't see her through the smoke."

"My hero version went something like: 'Keisha is a twenty-nine-year-old woman who discovered a painful truth about someone she loved. She sat with that truth, felt the full weight of it, and then stood up. She got tested. She found a therapist. She ended a relationship that wasn't honest. She rebuilt her confidence. And she decided that the rest of her life would be built on a foundation of truth, even when truth was harder than lies.' That's my story now. Not what happened to me. What I did about it."

The Women Who Came Before You

Before I close, I want to remind you of something that the isolation of this experience can make you forget: you are not the first. Thousands of women have walked this exact path, discovered their partner's involvement with a trans woman or femboy, processed the shock, navigated the shame, made the impossible decision, and rebuilt their lives. They are teachers, nurses, lawyers, hairstylists, accountants, pastors' wives, CEOs, and stay-at-home mothers. They are your age and your grandmother's age. They live in your city and in cities you've never visited. They are everywhere, and they are silent, because the stigma keeps them quiet.

But their silence doesn't mean they're absent. It means they're invisible. And one of the things this book hopes to change is that invisibility. Because when you can't see the women who came before you, you feel like you're walking a path that nobody has walked. And when you feel like nobody has walked the path, you feel like nobody understands. And when you feel like nobody understands, the loneliness becomes unbearable.

They understand. They are out there. And many of them would welcome the chance to tell you: "I made it through. So will you."

Final Voices

I asked several of the women in this book to share one sentence, just one, that they would say to a woman who is at the beginning of this journey. Here is what they said:

Francine (St. Louis, stayed): "The marriage on the other side of this, if you choose to stay, can be more real than anything you had before; but only if both of you are willing to be completely honest."

Nicole (Jacksonville, left): "Leaving was the hardest decision I ever made and the best decision I ever made, and both of those things are true at the same time."

Sandra (Houston, left): "Forgiveness is for you, not for him; but trust is earned, not owed, and you never have to give it again."

Tamara (Columbus, evolved): "The relationship you build after the truth can be stronger than the one you built before it; but it will never be the same, and you have to be okay with that."

Denitra (Cleveland, left): "The shame was never yours to carry, set it down and don't you dare pick it back up."

Michelle (Oakland, evolved): "Honesty is harder than secrecy, but honesty is the only thing that lets both of you breathe."

Lynn (Raleigh, left): "You are more than what happened to you, write your own list and prove it to yourself every day."

Tanya (Atlanta, left): "The first act of power is getting tested, it's the moment you stop being a victim and start being a woman who takes care of herself."

Paulette (Baltimore, stayed): "Find one person you can tell the whole truth to: the shame can't survive when it's spoken out loud."

Gail (Philadelphia, left): "The math has to work, if the numbers don't add up emotionally, financially, or physically, trust the math."

A Vision for a More Honest Culture

I began this book by telling you that it was going to be the most honest conversation you've ever had about male sexuality, Black masculinity, and the secret lives that flourish in the gap between desire and identity. I hope I've delivered on that promise. But I want to close by talking about what a world without that gap might look like.

Imagine a culture where a man could say, "I am attracted to femininity in many forms, including trans women," without losing his job, his church, or his family. Where that statement would be met not with disgust or pity but with the same shrug we give any other variation of human desire. Where a boy growing up could recognize his attraction without shame and develop the language to talk about it honestly, rather than burying it so deep that it erupts decades later in the form of a secret life that devastates everyone it touches.

In that world, there would be no DL. Not because the attraction would cease to exist, but because the secrecy would have no reason to exist. Men would be able to pursue their desires openly and honestly. Women would be able to make informed choices about who they partner with. Trans women and femboys would be able to have relationships in the light, not in the shadows. And the pain that has filled these twelve chapters: the lies, the discovery, the grief, the shame, the health scares, the impossible decisions, would simply not occur. Not because the desire was eliminated, but because the honesty was present from the beginning.

We are not there yet. We may not get there in our lifetime. But every honest conversation moves us closer. Every woman who refuses to carry a shame that doesn't belong to her moves us closer. Every man who finds the courage to tell the truth about who he is moves us closer. And this book, for all it's pain, is a step in that direction.

The change begins in small places. It begins when a mother tells her son that his feelings are valid, all of them, even the ones that don't fit the script. It begins when a pastor preaches compassion for the complexity of human desire instead of condemnation for it's expression. It begins when a woman tells her friend, "This happened to me, and I am not ashamed," and the friend responds with love instead of gossip. It begins when a man looks in the mirror and says, "I am what I am, and I can be honest about it," and the world does not punish him for his honesty.

These are small acts. But small acts, repeated across thousands of homes and churches and schools and communities, become a culture shift. And a culture shift is how the DL stops being necessary. Not by eliminating the desire: the desire is human and it will endure. But by eliminating the need to hide it. When hiding is no longer necessary, the secret life becomes unnecessary. And when the secret life becomes unnecessary, the devastation it causes ceases to exist.

That is the world I am working toward. Not because I am an optimist, I have seen too much pain in these pages to be naïve. But because I believe that truth, spoken clearly and compassionately, is the most powerful force available to human beings. And this book is my contribution to the truth.

Final Words

I want to close by speaking directly to you one last time. Not to the collective "you" that has filled these pages. To you: the specific woman holding this book right now, with your specific pain, your specific history, your specific questions about what comes next.

You are going to be okay. I know it doesn't feel that way right now. I know there are days when the weight of this experience makes it hard to breathe, hard to eat, hard to imagine a future that doesn't hurt. But every woman who has walked this path before you has arrived at the same destination: a life that is fuller, more honest, and more authentic than the one she had before the discovery. Not because the discovery was a gift: it wasn't. But because the process of surviving it revealed a version of herself that she didn't know existed. A version that is stronger, wiser, more compassionate, and more fiercely committed to living in the truth.

That version of you is already emerging. You can feel her in the moments when you set a boundary and hold it. In the moments when you look in the mirror and see not a woman who was deceived but a woman who survived deception. In the moments when you choose to move forward instead of looking back. She is you. She has always been you. The crisis didn't create her: it revealed her.

This book began with a secret. His secret. But it ends with yours: the secret knowledge that you are more resilient, more perceptive, and more powerful than you ever knew. That knowledge is yours now. Nobody can take it from you. Nobody can talk you out of it. It is the hard-won inheritance of the hardest experience of your life, and it belongs to you alone.

Go live your life. Not his. Not the life the culture says you should have. Not the life that was designed by someone else's lies. Your life. The one you are building right now, with every choice you make, every boundary you set, every morning you wake up and choose truth over comfort.

You are not what happened to you. You are what you choose to do next.

And whatever you choose, I am honored that you let me walk this road with you.

A Letter to the Reader

Dear Sister,

When I started writing this book, I didn't know if anyone would read it. The topic is one that most people avoid. The people involved are people most of the world wants to pretend don't exist. And the pain at the center of it, your pain, is a pain that our culture has decided is too complicated, too stigmatized, and too uncomfortable to address head-on.

But you read it. All of it. And in doing so, you have joined a quiet sisterhood of women who have refused to be silenced by stigma, refused to be diminished by shame, and refused to let someone else's choices define the limits of their lives. That sisterhood doesn't have a name, a meeting place, or a membership card. But it exists in every city, every church, every neighborhood where a woman has looked at the worst truth of her life and said: "I can survive this."

You can. And you will.

I wrote this book because I believe that no woman should have to navigate this experience without a map. The map is imperfect. Every woman's journey is different, and no book can anticipate every turn, every obstacle, every unexpected moment of grace or grief. But a map, even an imperfect one, is better than wandering in the dark. And you have been in the dark long enough.

As you close this book and return to your life, your real, messy, beautiful, painful, unfinished life, carry these things with you:

Carry the knowledge. You now understand more about this dynamic than most professionals. You understand the psychology, the mechanics, the cultural forces, the emotional landscape, and the health dimensions. That knowledge cannot be unlearned. It is yours forever, and it will protect you.

Carry the compassion. Not just for the other people in this dynamic, but for yourself. You have been through something that would break a lesser person. You are not broken. You are bruised, you are tired, you are angry, you are grieving; but you are not broken. Treat yourself with the same compassion you would give to any woman who came to you with this story. You deserve it.

Carry the conviction. The conviction that you are worthy of truth. That you are worthy of a partner who does not hide. That you are worthy of a life where you don't have to guess, investigate, or wonder. That conviction was shaken by this experience, but it was not destroyed. It is still there, waiting for you to reclaim it.

And carry the courage. The courage to tell your truth when you are ready. The courage to set boundaries that protect your peace. The courage to leave if leaving is right, to stay if staying is right, to evolve if evolution is right. The courage to build whatever comes next on the only foundation worth building on: honesty.

I don't know your name. I don't know your city, your age, your circumstances. I don't know whether you're at the beginning of this journey or years into it. But I know this: you are the woman this book was written for. Every sentence, every story, every statistic, every composite voice, all of it was written with you in mind. The specific, singular, irreplaceable you.

Thank you for trusting me with your pain. Thank you for staying through the hard parts. Thank you for being brave enough to read what most people look away from. And thank you for doing the one thing that every woman in this situation deserves to do but so few are given the tools to accomplish: understanding.

Understanding doesn't fix everything. But it changes everything. And you, having read this book, have been changed. Not into someone new. Into someone more. More informed. More prepared. More resilient. More yourself.

Go be that woman. The world needs her.

With love, respect, and unshakable belief in your strength,

The Author

BIBLIOGRAPHY

Bibliography

Apostolou, Menelaos, et al. "The Consequences of Infidelity: A Study of Emotional Reactions." Personality and Individual Differences, 191, 2022.

Barrett, Deirdre. Supernormal Stimuli: How Primal Urges Overran Their Evolutionary Purpose. W. W. Norton & Company, 2010.

Bozoyan, Christiane, & Schmiedeberg, Claudia. "The Consequences of Infidelity for Wellbeing." Journal of Social and Personal Relationships, 2022.

Browder, Brenda Stone. Diary of a Cover Girl: How I Survived the Down Low. OurPath, 2021.

Brown, Brené. Rising Strong: How the Ability to Reset Transforms the Way We Live, Love, Parent, and Lead. Random House, 2015.

Buss, David M. et al. "Sex Differences in Jealousy: Evolution, Physiology, and Psychology." Psychological Science, 3(4), 1992, 251-255.

Buss, David M. "Sex Differences in Jealousy: Evolution, Physiology, and Psychology." Psychological Science, 3(4), 1992, 251-255.

Carpenter, Christopher J. "Meta-Analyses of Sex Differences in Responses to Sexual Versus Emotional Infidelity." Psychology of Women Quarterly, 36(1), 2012, 25-37.

Centers for Disease Control and Prevention. "Fast Facts: HIV in the United States." CDC HIV Data and Statistics, 2024. https://www.cdc.gov/hiv/data-research/facts-stats/index.html

Centers for Disease Control and Prevention. "Guide to Taking a Sexual History." CDC Clinical Guidance, 2024.

Centers for Disease Control and Prevention. "Sexually Transmitted Infections Surveillance, 2024 (Provisional)." CDC, September 2025.

Centers for Disease Control and Prevention. "STI Screening Recommendations." CDC Clinical Guidance, 2021.

Centers for Disease Control and Prevention. "The Impact of HIV on Black People in the United States." KFF (Kaiser Family Foundation), 2024. https://www.kff.org/hiv-aids/the-impact-of-hiv-on-black-people-in-the-united-states/

Chu, S. Y. Peterman, T. A. Doll, L. S. Buehler, J. W. & Curran, J. W. "AIDS in Bisexual Men in the United States: Epidemiology and Transmission to Women." American Journal of Epidemiology, 135(7), 1992, 750-758.

Couples Therapy Inc. "Emotional Affairs: Gender Differences, Relationship Impact, and Contemporary Research." CouplesTherapyInc.com, 2025.

Denizet-Lewis, Benoit. "Double Lives on the Down Low." The New York Times Magazine, August 3, 2003.

Diamond, Lisa M. Sexual Fluidity: Understanding Women's Love and Desire. Harvard University Press, 2009.

Freyd, Jennifer J. Klest, Bridget, & Allard, Carolyn B. "Betrayal Trauma: Relationship to Physical Health, Psychological Distress, and a Written Disclosure Intervention." Journal of Trauma & Dissociation, 6(3), 2005, 83-104.

Gordon, Kristina Coop, & Mitchell, Erica A. "Infidelity in the Time of COVID-19." Family Process, 59(3), 2020, 956-966.

Gordon, Kristina Coop, Baucom, Donald H. & Snyder, Douglas K. "An Integrative Intervention for Promoting Recovery from Extramarital Affairs." Journal of Marital and Family Therapy, 30(2), 2004, 213-231.

Gottman, John M. & Silver, Nan. What Makes Love Last? How to Build Trust and Avoid Betrayal. Simon & Schuster, 2012.

Grov, Christian, Breslow, Aaron S. Newcomb, Michael E. Rosenberger, Joshua G. & Bauermeister, José A. "Gay and Bisexual Men's Use of the Internet: Research from the 1990s through 2013." Journal of Sex Research, 51(4), 2014, 390-409.

Grov, Christian, et al. "Perceived Consequences of Casual Online Sexual Activities on Heterosexual Relationships: A U. S. Online Survey." Archives of Sexual Behavior, 40(2), 2011, 429-439.

Herman, Judith. Trauma and Recovery: The Aftermath of Violence. Basic Books, 2015 (revised edition).

hooks, bell. All About Love: New Visions. William Morrow, 2000.

Hsu, Kevin J. et al. "Who Are Gynandromorphophilic Men?" Psychological Medicine, 46(4), 2016, 819-827.

Hsu, Kevin J. Rosenthal, A. M. Miller, David I. & Bailey, J. Michael. "Who Are Gynandromorphophilic Men? Characterizing Men with Sexual Interest in Transgender Women." Psychological Medicine, 46(4), 2016, 819-827. doi:10.1017/S0033291715002317

Hufstetler, Kaitlin, et al. "Clinical Updates in Sexually Transmitted Infections, 2024." PMC/Clinical Obstetrics and Gynecology, 2024.

IMPACT Psychological Services. "Why Does Betrayal Hurt So Much? Understanding the Psychology of Broken Trust." Impact-Psych.com, November 2025.

Kaiser Family Foundation. "The Impact of HIV on Women in the United States." KFF, 2024. https://www.kff.org/hiv-aids/the-impact-of-hiv-on-women-in-th

e-united-states/

King, J. L. (with Karen Hunter). On the Down Low: A Journey into the Lives of "Straight" Black Men Who Sleep with Men. Broadway Books, 2004.

Kinsey, Alfred C. Pomeroy, Wardell B. & Martin, Clyde E. Sexual Behavior in the Human Male. W. B. Saunders, 1948.

Kinsey, Alfred C. Pomeroy, Wardell B. Martin, Clyde E. & Gebhard, Paul H. Sexual Behavior in the Human Female. W. B. Saunders, 1953.

Ko, Amy J. "The Price of a Gender Transition: Costs, Insurance, and Health Equity." Medium, 2021.

Lex LGBT. "Best Trans Dating Apps for 2025." Lex.lgbt, July 2025.

Lonergan, Marianne, et al. "Is Romantic Partner Betrayal a Form of Traumatic Experience?" Stress and Health, 37(1), 2021, 19-31.

Lonergan, Marianne, et al. "Physical Symptoms of Infidelity: A Qualitative Investigation." Journal of Health Psychology, 2021.

Lonergan, Marianne, O'Connor, Cliodhna, & Lotmore, Aisling. "Physical Symptoms of Infidelity: A Qualitative Investigation." Journal of Health Psychology, 2021.

Macapagal, Kathryn, Moskowitz, David A. Li, Dennis H. & Carrion, Andres. "Hookup App Use, Sexual Behavior, and Sexual Health Among Adolescent Men Who Have Sex with Men in the United States." Journal of Adolescent Health, 62(6), 2018, 708-715. doi:10.1016/j.jadohealth.2018.01.001

McCree, Donna Hubbard, et al. "Disparities in Incidence of Human Immunodeficiency Virus Infection Among Black and White Women, United States, 2010-2016." Morbidity and Mortality Weekly Report (MMWR), 68(18), 2019, 416-418. doi:10.15585/mmwr.mm6818a3

Millett, Gregorio A. Peterson, John L. Wolitski, Richard J. & Stall, Ron. "Greater Risk for HIV Infection of Black Men Who Have Sex with Men: A Critical

Literature Review." American Journal of Public Health, 96(6), 2006, 1007-1019.

Ms. Magazine. "The Cost of Being Myself: Cosmetics and Gender-Affirming Care." Ms. Magazine, May 28, 2024.

Neu, Natalie, et al. "Updates on Testing, Treatment, and Prevention of Sexually Transmitted Infections in the United States, 2025." PMC, 2025.

Operario, Don, Burton, Jaime, Underhill, Kristen, & Sevelius, Jae. "Men Who Have Sex with Transgender Women: Challenges to Category-Based HIV Prevention." AIDS and Behavior, 12(1), 2008, 18-25.

Operario, Don, et al. "Men Who Have Sex with Transgender Women: Challenges to Category-Based HIV Prevention." AIDS and Behavior, 12(1), 2008, 18-25.

Ortman, Dennis. Transcending Post-Infidelity Stress Disorder. Celestial Arts, 2009.

Ortman, Dennis. "Post-Infidelity Stress Disorder." 2009.

Padula, William V. Heru, Shiona, & Campbell, Jonathan D. "Societal Implications of Health Insurance Coverage for Medically Necessary Services in the U. S. Transgender Population." Journal of General Internal Medicine, 31(4), 2016, 394-397.

Paz-Bailey, Gabriela, et al. "Trends in Internet Use Among Men Who Have Sex with Men." JAIDS, 75(Suppl 3), 2017, S288, S295.

Paz-Bailey, Gabriela, Hoots, Brooke E. Xia, Ming, et al. "Trends in Internet Use Among Men Who Have Sex with Men in the United States." Journal of Acquired Immune Deficiency Syndromes, 75(Suppl 3), 2017, S288, S295.

Perel, Esther. The State of Affairs: Rethinking Infidelity. Harper, 2017.

Petterson, Lanna J. & Vasey, Paul L. "Heterosexual Men's Pupillary Responses to Stimuli Depicting Cisgender Males, Cisgender Females, and

Gynandromorphs." Biological Psychology, 178, 2023, 108531. doi:10.1016/j.biopsycho.2023.108531

Pornhub Insights. "The 2022 Year in Review." Pornhub.com, December 2022.

Pornhub Insights. "The 2023 Year in Review." Pornhub.com, December 2023.

Pornhub Insights. "The 2025 Year in Review." Pornhub.com, December 2025.

POZ Magazine. "The Oprah Winfrey Show Discusses the 'Down Low.'" POZ, April 16, 2024. https://www.poz.com/article/oprah-winfrey-show-discusses-low

Psychology Today. "Emotional Infidelity: A Woman's Perspective." Psychology Today, August 2023.

Psychology Today. "The Financial Costs of Gender Transition." Psychology Today, September 14, 2019.

Roamers Therapy. "Exploring Infidelity as a Trauma: Understanding Its Psychological Impact." RoamersTherapy.com, November 2025.

Rosenthal, A. M. Hsu, Kevin J. & Bailey, J. Michael. "Who Are Gynandromorphophilic Men? An Internet Survey of Men with Sexual Interest in Transgender Women." Archives of Sexual Behavior, 46(1), 2017, 255-264. doi:10.1007/s10508-016-0872-6

Sidari, J. "The Kinsey Scale Is Ill-Suited to Most Sexuality Research Because It Does Not Measure a Single Construct." Proceedings of the National Academy of Sciences, 117(44), 2020, 27080. doi:10.1073/pnas.2015820117

Spring, Janis Abrahms. After the Affair: Healing the Pain and Rebuilding Trust. William Morrow, 2012 (revised edition).

Sullivan, Patrick S. Khosropour, Christine M. Luber, Nicholas, et al. "A Comparison of Sexual Behavior Patterns Among Men Who Have Sex with Men and Heterosexual Men and Women." Journal of Acquired Immune Deficiency Syndromes, 60(1), 2012, 83-90.

doi:10.1097/QAI.0b013e318247925e

Taimi. "Transgender Dating & LGBTQ+ Social Network." Taimi.com, 2025.

Tompkins, Avery. "There's No Chasing Involved: Cis/Trans Relationships, 'Tranny Chasers,' and the Future of a Sex-Positive Trans Politics." Journal of Homosexuality, 61(5), 2014, 766-780.

TransVitae. "Best Dating Apps for Trans People: The 2025 Safety Guide." TransVitae.com, June 2025.

van der Kolk, Bessel. The Body Keeps the Score: Brain, Mind, and Body in the Healing of Trauma. Penguin Books, 2014.

Washington City Paper. "20 Trans Dating Apps and Sites in 2026." Washington City Paper, December 2025.

Washington City Paper. "The Down Low Today." Washington City Paper, 2023.

Weinberg, Martin S. & Williams, Colin J. "Men Sexually Interested in Transwomen (MSTW): Gendered Embodiment and the Construction of Sexual Desire." Journal of Sex Research, 47(4), 2010, 374-383. doi:10.1080/00224490903050568

Winfrey, Oprah. "Free from Life on the Down Low." The Oprah Winfrey Show (Episode aired October 7, 2010). https://www.oprah.com/oprahshow/free-from-life-on-the-down-low/all

Workowski, Kimberly A. et al. "Sexually Transmitted Infections Treatment Guidelines, 2021." MMWR Recommendations and Reports, 70(No. RR-4), 2021, 1-187.